A GARDEN'S PURPOSE

FÉLIX DE ROSEN

A GARDEN'S PURPOSE

Cultivating Our Connection with the Natural World

PA PRESS

PRINCETON ARCHITECTURAL PRESS · NEW YORK

me enseñaste a amar con valentía,
lo sabes?
tu corazón de azúcar de sandía
baila en las palabras de este libro.
mafe, esto es para todas las flores
con las que somos tan afortunados
de compartir la vida

you taught me how to love with courage,
you know that?
your watermelon sugar heart
dances in the words of this book
mafe, here's to all the flowers
that we are so lucky to share life with

CONTENTS

PART THREE

HABITAT

DESIGN WITH NATURE

At the time of this writing, you and I are two individuals on a planet of eight billion human beings. That's four times more than a century ago. The human footprint has grown so much there is no place untouched by us anymore. Our communications and transportation networks crisscross the planet, microplastics end up in the tissue of deep ocean fish, and even supposedly *wild* places like national parks are heavily monitored by humans.

It's easy to shrug our shoulders and lament the "end of nature." But nature is not ending, and the planet will endure regardless of human actions. Nor is human impact on the environment new: we have been shaping our environment for tens of thousands of years, by hunting, foraging, and making tools. But whereas indigenous ways of life tended to cooperate with nature, modern day capitalism works, primarily, by exploiting it, by taking without giving. Can we assume responsibility for our oversized impact on the natural world and give back what we've taken? What models do we have to inspire long-term, symbiotic interaction with our homelands? Where do we start?

Gardens are places where we decide, intentionally, to interact and cooperate with the living forces of nature. They include the residential gardens, community gardens, and parks that we know well. But other places can be gardens too: farms, forests, urban courtyards, high-rise balconies, sidewalk strips, entire cities, and landscapes. To really understand this, we need to forget everything we know about what a garden is. I invite you on a journey to rediscover gardens as places where we build and nurture diverse, meaningful, and mutually beneficial relationships with the living world.

The word *garden* is full of intimidating and inaccessible ideas and images. But everybody has a deep spiritual connection to the Earth, so everybody can garden. This book does not prescribe any specific way of gardening. It's not a DIY handbook because everybody's spirit and situation are different. Some live in cold climates, others in the tropics. Some have access to resources; others don't. This book focuses on the inspiring qualities that all gardens share: wonder, design, and habitat.

In part one—"Wonder"—we develop a new way of looking at the world in which every place is a potential garden, from a driveway to an abandoned parking lot to an urban plaza. We quickly learn that gardens have as many looks and colors as there are different types of people. But they are all crafted with a desire to make a place unique and special, whether by providing refuge, growing food, or building community. That desire acts like magic—making gardens wonder-filled places to be.

In part two—"Design"—we look at the physical materials that shape a garden. Walls, fences, and paths; paved areas and rest areas; and pots and planters all help create the backbone of a garden. They guide our experience. A path invites us forward; a fence stops us. A creative paving pattern imbues a space with dynamism. But it's not just about look and feel. The materials we use have impact beyond the boundaries of the garden. They come from other places, from mines, forests, and riverbanks,

LEFT
Gardens are defined by
their difference from their
surroundings, as is visible in
this experimental garden plot
in Los Angeles.

RIGHT
We care for gardens and
they in turn take care of us.
A wild-looking garden design
by Wagon Landscaping grows
through the asphalt of an
abandoned parking lot in the
suburbs of Paris.

some nearby and others far away. They can invite people and
wildlife into the garden or repel them, and our design decisions
determine our collective pressure on the environment.

In part three—"Habitat"—we consider the garden as a living, breathing entity that changes over time. From the microbial activity in the soil, to the growth of plants and the changes
in the weather and seasons, gardens are alive. We understand
these changes better through patient, consistent observation,
allowing us to work *with* the garden instead of *on* the garden.
If we do this well, we realize that we are never gardening alone,
but rather in collaboration with all that is alive around us. And
we start to understand that we too are a crucial part of the rambunctious river of life.

Each chapter in the book is dedicated to a specific element
of the garden or a related and essential theme. There is some
overlap between the chapters because these themes, or subjects, are as interconnected as the garden itself. There are also
some rather important subjects that are not included, such
as lighting, moon cycles, edible crops, and fungi. Instead of
covering every possible subject, this book focuses on simple
stories to inspire others to initiate their own experiments
and interventions.

A few basic values and beliefs run throughout the book. Although they will become obvious as we read on, it's worth stating them explicitly because they are important and deserve clarity.

First, *we humans are a part of nature, not apart from it.* Western civilization has long imagined nature as something "out there," away from humans. This gap between nature and culture emerged partly as a way to justify the exploitation of nature. And it's clearly seen in our cities, which, for the most part, are not well integrated within the landscape. But no matter how much we isolate ourselves, our homes, and our cities from the surrounding ecosystem, nature always find a way back in: dandelions grow in the cracks of the pavement, birds nest underneath eaves, and even the most housebound among us feel relief from a fresh cool breeze. That's because we humans, as well as our cities and homes, are dependent on the natural world. We are physically and spiritually connected with it, and the garden is one of the many places where we cultivate that bond.

Second, *every single person on this planet is part of nature.* Everybody belongs and has an innate connection to the Earth, which they can express through the process of gardening. This book does not prescribe a singular approach to gardening because no garden should look alike. The case studies featured in the following pages include projects by famous landscape architects, traditional practices of indigenous cultures, and crafty DIY solutions arrived at by people without formal training. In addressing the challenges of our world, we need top-down interventions by governments and international organizations, but we also need a bottom-up, people driven revolution in the way we relate to our Earth and its many-hued landscapes. One residential garden will not solve the climate emergency, but a joyful, life-affirming, and colorful gardening movement will. It's that ground-up earthquake that this book intends to fuel.

Third, *what we do unto others, we do to ourselves.* We don't always have to get along with other species, but we absolutely

OPPOSITE, TOP
Nature is everywhere, but do we know how to look? Dozens of plant species make a home on a missing piece of pavement in Salinas, California.

OPPOSITE, BOTTOM
Can "trash" and other abundant materials compose a garden? Metal cans are repurposed as miniature planters in this garden at the International Garden Festival at Chaumont-sur-Loire, France.

and unconditionally must recognize their agency and right to live. It is even in our own self-interest. Animals, plants, fungi, and everything that has life force are part of our interdependent planetary community. Anthropocentrism, the view that humans are the most important members of that community, is objectively wrong: our survival depends on others. The photosynthetic cells of plants are actively producing the oxygen that is keeping us alive at this very moment. Ecocentrism, the view that prioritizes whole ecosystems instead of individual parts, recognizes how radically interdependent we are. Gardens are places of cooperation and symbiosis, where we can build the ecocentric world we dream of.

Fourth, *resourcefulness is more important than resources*. A garden does not require a landscape architect or a fancy designer. It does not require a unique plant specimen or concrete pavers. It requires creativity. Every place is abundant with *something*. We just have to look and find that something. Easy access to store-bought materials can be an obstacle to our imagination. Concrete is unappealing not because of its heavy environmental costs, but because it's boring: its easy availability gives us an excuse to overlook what's right in front of our eyes. A garden made of local resources is grounded in the qualities that make a place unlike any other.

Fifth, *observation is care*. We cannot know our surroundings without dedicating attention to it. Unbelievably rich details emerge when we sit or kneel in front of a meadow, or a stream, or an urban sidewalk and quietly, patiently observe. Which insects and plants are present? Where are they present? The details become more complex when we observe over weeks, months, and years. How is an insect population responding to changes in weather? Which mushroom species appear repeatedly underneath that tree? Why is that plant healthy but another plant of the species dying? There is no point in intervening, in designing, if we don't know what we're designing with. That's what observation teaches us.

Sixth, *we define beauty*. Forgetting what we know about gardens means ditching the stereotyped images we have of

them. Ecocentric, resourceful gardens can challenge conventional notions of pretty and beautiful. They might look a little wilder, messier, and scrappier. They might, in fact, totally shock us…at first. By expanding our notions of beauty to include new values—like reusing materials, the dignity of other species, and community participation—we open the door to a radical reimagination of our gardens, landscapes, and lifestyles.

As magical spaces, gardens fill us with hope and wonder. As gathering places, they nurture friendships and communities. Thoughtfully crafted, they make us pause and appreciate our surroundings. Full of edible plants, they nourish us. Full of diversity—human and nonhuman—they connect us with the polychromatic world in which we live. They make us feel at home in our own bodies, in our cities, and on our planet. The garden is a powerful, generous way of looking at the world because, in the words of Wendell Berry, "A garden is a solution that leads to other solutions. It is part of the limitless pattern of good health and good sense."

PART ONE

WONDER

CHAPTER ONE

GARDENS ARE EVERYWHERE

Ryoanji is a Zen Buddhist temple on the outskirts of Kyoto, Japan. In a space that measures thirty feet by seventy-five feet, fifteen stones sit on white gravel. When looking at the garden from any angle on the ground, only fourteen of the stones are ever visible. The inability to see all the stones at once communicates the Zen belief that reality cannot be fully understood, only contemplated, appreciated, and loved. The wall on two sides of the garden is made of clay, stained brown and orange with age, and helps frame this meditative space. Ryoanji is known as a garden, but apart from the mosses and lichens on the stones, there are no plants. So what makes it a garden?

Gardens are physical spaces designed with a caring intention. The walls that enclose Ryoanji mark this is as a meditative space, not better or worse than the surrounding landscape, just different. That intention separates the garden from its surroundings and tells a story at the same time. Formal gardens designed around harmonious proportions might share a story of neatness and order as important societal values. Botanical gardens might demonstrate biodiversity as a value. Ryoanji shares a belief that the world is always more than we think it is and so is always full of wonder.

A garden's message, its intention, is communicated through space. The true diversity of gardens comes from unique dreams and desires expressed through a variety of spaces. And yet, popular culture simplifies that diversity into stereotypical garden imagery. Can we let go of what we think gardens are and start seeing gardens everywhere?

We commonly associate gardens with enjoyment and re-laxation. Put simply, we feel good in gardens. There are many reasons for this, but they can be summarized by the idea of biophilia, namely that human beings have a deep, evolution-ary affinity for nature and the outdoors. As enjoyable spaces, gardens are also important social spaces, for families, friends, and the wider community.

Plants play many different roles in gardens. They can be primarily ornamental, meant to impress, comfort, and sur-prise, and they, of course, have practical purposes too, such as producing food via vegetable and herb gardens and farms. Increasingly, ornamental gardens in both the US and Europe are looking to incorporate harvestable plants into their spaces. In botanical gardens, plants play a pedagogical role, educating the public and serving as a living library.

Gardens are healing because they connect people to na-ture, whether that nature is of the outdoor variety or the inner spiritual variety. Some gardens are specifically intended for the healing of disease or trauma. Hospitals increasingly fea-ture spaces where patients can enjoy vegetation and fresh air. Garden making by individuals and communities can emerge from a deep need for expression. Community gardens in mar-ginalized communities assert the power, dignity, and history of the community. For immigrants, gardens are places to grow the foods of their homeland. In the United States, gardens run by indigenous communities assert their caretakers' living tradi-tions and spiritual connection to land.

OPPOSITE, TOP
Gardens communicate an intention through space. An experimental garden plot in Los Angeles by Terremoto uses dune fencing to mark off the garden from its surroundings.

OPPOSITE, BOTTOM
What roles do plants play in a garden? In this garden in Salinas, California, a hedge of California natives provides habitat for insects and separates the vegetable crops inside the garden from the street. Palms and agaves add punch to the scene.

Gardens are not always intended for people. Some, like pollinator gardens, may focus on providing habitat for wildlife. Or they may recognize plants and animals as collaborators in the design process. The French landscape architect Gilles Clément developed a practice of designing around the spontaneous movement of plants and animals in the garden: animals carry seeds in their droppings, winds blow seeds around, and plants can spread underground via roots and shoots. Clément observed these spontaneous processes and integrated them into his design process.

Gardens are always political spaces in the sense that they put forward a set of beliefs and values about the world. The enormous gardens at Versailles, outside of Paris, tell us a lot about how the French monarchy saw itself in the seventeenth century: infinitely powerful, harmonious, generous. All public gardens—whether it's the White House Rose Garden or Central Park—are built on a set of beliefs about what society should look like. But just as they are symbols for those in power,

ABOVE
British artist Derek Jarman built his famous gravel garden at Prospect Cottage partly as a way to cope with the grief of his AIDS diagnosis.

OPPOSITE
We can never fully predict or control the growth of other living beings, including humans and plants. A mix of species sown by seed and others brought in by animals, and the air, grow in this garden on a former parking lot in suburban Paris.

OPPOSITE, TOP
A dandelion (*Taraxacum officinale*) grows in the cracks between brick, concrete, and stone. Is this a garden?

OPPOSITE, LEFT
A small street fence in Berlin keeps pets and people out and signals that this is a cared for space.

OPPOSITE, RIGHT
A narrow strip between sidewalk and fence offers an explosion of colors and smells for humans and nonhumans alike in Salinas, California.

gardens are also places that nurture rebellion and innovation. At the Princess Gardens in Berlin, local residents interested in cultivating more progressive societal models grow vegetables and hold workshops on everything from pickling to alternative currencies.

These are just a few of the intentions that inspire people around the world to create what we call gardens. But where do gardens grow? Let's start small and local. Look around your neighborhood and notice what grows in the cracks in the pavement, asphalt, and walls. These tiny worlds are crafted by plants and home to diverse wildlife. Only a small shift in our perspective enables us to see these as gardens.

Next, there are all the spaces that exist around roads and transportation areas: sidewalk medians, road buffers, and the ground alongside train tracks. These are often forgotten because of their small size or their inconvenient location, but they have the advantage of being everywhere, and all those small spaces add up to a lot of acreage in the end.

Buildings and the spaces around them provide ample opportunities for gardens: balconies, rooftops, narrow alleyways between buildings, interior courtyards, and indoor spaces all provide the possibility—if we want it—to bring gardens to our homes and workplaces.

Yards, parks, and community gardens are the most well-known garden spaces. Their size and layout depends on the way we build our cities, towns, and homes. In the US, homes are on average larger and spread farther apart than homes in Europe. As a result, cities and suburbs in the US have a lot of potential gardening space in between buildings, much of it unused or covered in lawn. European urban areas are denser, with community gardens generally located on the outskirts.

Some city governments around the globe, however, are using the garden as a model for urban policy and development. In Costa Rica, the city of Curridabat developed the Sweet City program, in which gardens and planted spaces are integrated into the fabric of the city, and where important pollinators such as bats and bees are given real citizenship status. These initiatives can have a massive impact on people's lives because they expand the garden to the scale of the city.

A garden can also be an entire landscape. Indeed, for cultures that have traditionally relied on harvesting wild plants, the plants in the landscape were looked after (e.g., by not overharvesting) and the landscape itself was managed (e.g., by practices such as controlled burns). This is the garden as landscape. Cooperation between political leaders, scientists, schools, families, and citizens can also cultivate gardening at the scale of the landscape: when one person plants a pollinator garden, it may appear pointless. But when many people start gardens in their homes, on sidewalk medians, and in school yards, it sets a new standard that changes everything from air quality to the availability of healthy food and the presence of wildlife. Western culture has often misunderstood nature and wilderness as being "out there," away from our cities. The reality is that we create nature by working with it in our gardens, cities, and landscapes.

Moving up in scale, we realize that the Earth itself is a garden. Gardens are places to care for. Gardening, as a model, is an antidote to the societally dominant model of extraction and consumption. No place on the planet is untouched by human influence; we can't change that at this point. Here's the real question: What can that influence look and feel like? The garden is both a place and a framework to answer this question. Hopefully, the gardens in this book can open up all the possible ways forward.

OPPOSITE, TOP
Can a city be a garden? The belief that nature and culture are separate has led to black-and-white divisions between human settlement and garden.

OPPOSITE, BOTTOM
"The most beautiful gardens I have ever seen are pristine coral reefs in the South Pacific." —Ian L. McHarg, *The Meaning of Gardens*

CHAPTER TWO

FROM ART IN THE GARDEN TO ART AS THE GARDEN

OPPOSITE, TOP
Inspired by the way the male satin bowerbird collects blue objects for its courting ritual, the Blue Desire garden at Chaumont-sur-Loire, France, turns discarded objects into art.

OPPOSITE, BOTTOM
Plants with blue undertones—including Mediterranean spurge (*Euphorbia characias* 'Glacier Blue'), lamb's ears (*Stachys byzantina* 'Silver Carpet'), blue fescue (*Festuca glauca*), wormwood (*Artemisia* 'Powis Castle')—complement the blue objects in the Blue Desire garden.

Every summer, Chaumont-sur-Loire, a commune and town in France's Loire Valley, hosts an international garden festival, where accepted applicants from all over the world prepare gardens that are open to the public. In the summer of 2021, one of these gardens, Blue Desire, offered a surprise. Various shades of blue make their way through the foliage of short trees at the perimeter of the garden. Moving past the trees on a path of decomposed granite, we arrive at the heart of the garden: a simple circle, roughly twenty feet in diameter, filled with trash. Jerry cans, fishing nets, tubes, shipping crates, chairs, skis, bottles, cups, and children's toys—all scattered around haphazardly, and all in different tones of blue. Amid the rubble are Mediterranean spurge, wormwood, lamb's ears, blue fescue, and other plants—all chosen for their blue undertones. The garden takes discarded everyday objects and makes them beautiful. A discarded shipping crate, if left on a sidewalk, looks like trash. But placed next to euphorbia with similar hues, we see it anew.

The garden's message is loud and clear: we live our lives surrounded with objects whose easy availability makes it painless for us to throw them away without thinking twice. By placing discarded objects at the heart of the garden, the designers offered a positive message: our everyday objects, including trash, are valuable. As in the garden, so can it be in life. We can develop more awareness of the ways we consume and produce material goods, and reframe our whole approach to consumption.

The garden was inspired by the courting rituals of the satin bowerbird. The male bird of this species gathers natural and human-made objects to build a "bower" to attract a female. Curiously, the bird loves to collect blue materials. Although the Blue Desire garden is not attempting to attract a mate, it seduces us by making us wonder: What new worlds are possible when we shift the way we relate to objects?

If art is the expression of emotion that imagines something new from what is given, then Blue Desire is both a garden and an artwork. We can have art in the garden, as in a sculpture or a beautiful paving pattern, but this limits our thinking of art to objects and materials. Could the entire garden, and the whole process of designing and nurturing a garden, be a form of art making? Gardens invite us to reflect, rest, play, and look at the world in a new way. Can they also be opportunities to explore and express our unique personality? Can the garden be a place where we nurture the relationships and ecosystems of our dreams?

Few people understand the garden as a place to explore and dream as fearlessly as artist Marcia Donahue in Berkeley, California. You know you're up for something special even from the street outside her home. Her house is screened by aloes, fan palms, Mexican weeping bamboo, and a eucalyptus tree, which is wrapped with what looks like a giant wooden necklace. Stone sculptures peek from behind the foliage.

Moving on a brick path from the sidewalk to the side of the house, we pass through an old wooden gate into a different dimension. Long vertical pole-like sculptures stand at angles,

OPPOSITE
Marcia Donahue's garden begins at the sidewalk, where ceramic necklaces—inspired by Buddhist *mala* beads—drape around a eucalyptus tree.

intermingling with tall, tropical-looking vegetation. The sculptures are actually ceramic pieces—spheres and pipes threaded over metal rebar. In a variation on these vertical pieces, Donahue also strings ceramic beads onto wire to create a set of oversized beads, inspired by the mala beads used by Hindus and Buddhists to recite mantras. There are also sculptures of friendly looking spirits, inspired by *nats*, or spirits, worshipped by Buddhists in Myanmar.

The exuberance of plants and objects in Donahue's garden create a feeling of total immersion. The density of the space makes it feel much larger than it actually is.

OVERLEAF, PAGE 38
Playful vertical sculptures add color and mystery to Donahue's garden.

OVERLEAF, PAGE 39, TOP LEFT
Nature and sculpture are hard to distinguish in Donahue's garden.

OVERLEAF, PAGE 39, TOP RIGHT
Broken bits of pottery, bricks, and glass offer a colorful, crunchy path in Donahue's Berkeley garden.

OVERLEAF, PAGE 39, BOTTOM
As if Donahue's garden couldn't get any better, the pack of heirloom chickens arrive. Cautious but friendly, they make the space feel more alive.

Objects are everywhere—some found, others crafted, some clearly visible, others hidden behind plants. The exuberance of plants and objects crammed in such a small place (forty feet by sixty feet) means that Donahue's garden is a place to pause and observe small details. Sometimes, the line between sculpture and plant is hard to differentiate. Donahue uses ceramics to create incredibly convincing replicas of botanical forms. A glazed ceramic bamboo shoot rises next to a Himalayan blue bamboo plant; I have to touch both to tell them apart.

Many of the objects are found and recycled. Friends have been giving Donahue bowling balls for years. She has placed some on her staircase, stabilized in pots and saucers. Others serve as groundcover, as if a strange bird were laying eggs there. One pathway is covered with pottery shards and tumbled glass—as I step on it, the sound is full of texture.

Donahue's various objects never feel out of place; they don't compete with the plants but complement each other. This process, Donahue tells me, didn't happen overnight, but piecemeal over time. It's impossible to design a garden like this in one go. It has to evolve organically. And as if things couldn't be even more wonderful, a gang of small, energetic heirloom chickens make a home of the garden.

Donahue's garden is inspiring and filled with infinite creative potential, one plant, one sculpture, one bowling ball at a time. It is a reminder to stop censoring and stifling ourselves, to explore and play. Donahue explains: "I really don't know what some of the conventions are, or I'm so bored by them that I have ignored them. But also, I've been doing this for a long time and it kind of builds. I've gotten away with this, I've gotten away with that. I can wear my glitter suit tonight. Nothing bad has happened. Good things have happened to me when I do what I want to do." This book explores many approaches to garden making. The goal is not to replicate them, but rather to inspire wonder and courage in others. Donahue's experience proves that the only rules worth following are the ones we create for ourselves.

ABOVE
Objects and plants don't compete in Donahue's garden. Giant pink feet echo the pink edges of cordyline (*Cordyline* 'Electric Flash').

OPPOSITE
Blue bowling balls and Donahue's ceramic poles complement each other in front of the spacious chicken coop.

Although her garden is on private property, Donahue opens it to the public every Sunday. She sees this as a way to give back to the community: "So even if I don't feel like it, I'm out there sweeping the paths and I'm grateful for that. It helps me get out there and stay in touch…This helps keep me plugged into the cycle of my garden, this weekly cycle of preparing it for others."

She continues, "Some people are scared of opening their private home to 'the public.' That's a scary thing for some people, but nobody has plundered my treasures. Somebody did fall in the pond once." Donahue's garden shows us that we can follow our gut and think outside the garden box. Surely the world will thank us for it.

PART TWO

DESIGN

CHAPTER THREE

THE FENCE—
SETTING AND UPSETTING
BOUNDARIES

OPPOSITE, TOP
A wooden fence harmonizes
gracefully with knife-leaf wattle
(*Acacia cultriformis*) and Pisa
conebush (*Leucadendron*
'Pisa') at Terremoto's Glen Oaks
site.

OPPOSITE, BOTTOM
A low white wall separates
a garden from the street in
Salinas, California. From left to
right are Mediterranean cypress
(*Cupressus sempervirens*),
Pampas grass (*Cortaderia
selloana*), and an olive tree
(*Olea europaea*).

I enjoy looking at people's gardens when I walk around the
suburbs near my home in Oakland. For the most part, people
in the Bay Area really care for their gardens. Plants from many
different climates flourish here in the mild climate and moist
coastal air, and the good weather makes it easy to garden year
round. It's interesting to see how people separate their gardens
from their neighbor's. In some instances, it's separated by a
wooden fence or a chain-link, or by a planted hedge. In others,
no divider at all exists, and you can step from one garden to
the next.

Boundaries say so much about what we think a garden is
in the first place. Is it a private fortress or a gathering place for
the community? Is the garden connected physically to other
gardens and the wider landscape, or is it an island unto itself?

The etymological roots of the word *garden* mean to enclose
or define. A garden is a space purposefully set apart from its
surroundings. It has a boundary, which physically and symbol-
ically demarcates it from its surroundings. That boundary may

be intentional, like a fence, or it may be unintentional, like an overgrown thicket at the end of a yard.

Michele Shelor is a landscape architect based in Phoenix, Arizona. To mark off one edge of her garden, Shelor planted a line of ocotillo plants. Ocotillo is thorny succulent, native to the southwestern US, that grows very tall and produces brilliant red flowers. Indigenous people in its native range have long used it as a fence, among other purposes.

Shelor's ocotillo fence shows that a garden can be built from local natural resources and inspired by local indigenous practices. This is a living fence, made of plants that get taller, stronger, and thornier over time. The fence requires minimal irrigation and leafs out when the seasonal rains come. Over time, the plants may die and need to be replaced, reminding us that the garden is something that must be nurtured and culti-vated, not simply taken for granted. The gaps in the fence are too small to allow a person through but big enough for some-one to peek out of and for small wildlife to move through. The fence signifies a boundary, but it also makes the garden part of the landscape, not apart from it.

In another part of the same garden, Shelor opted for a more human-made boundary. This fence is composed of iron poles emerging from the ground without horizontal pieces to support it. The clear, simple geometry is elegant, and the transparency makes it enjoyable to look at. Unlike the ocotillo, the iron poles are made of nonrenewable metal, mined and shipped from far away. Like the ocotillo, the iron poles mark the boundary of the garden without shutting off the surround-ing landscape.

These are just two examples of fences, which are both visual and physical barriers that provide privacy and security. Fences can be see-through or completely opaque, blocking wildlife from coming in and out of the garden, and cutting off neighbors from one another.

Fences can be modified with holes and passages at their base to allow ground dwelling mammals like possums and raccoons to move through. Wildlife live in our gardens too, and

OPPOSITE
Ocotillo cacti (*Fouquieria splendens*) compose Michele Shelor's living fence. During the seasonal rains, the whole fence leafs out.

A GARDEN'S PURPOSE

our fences can help facilitate their freedom of movement. As we'll discuss more in chapters thirteen and fourteen, allowing light, air, pollen, and wildlife through a garden boundary connects that garden to the surrounding landscape, making it a more spontaneous and dynamic place.

Wood is the most common material used for fences, and historically, vertical slats have been the norm. Recently, however, horizontal slat fences have become more popular (these have an interesting look: the horizontal lines of the fence run parallel to the ground plane as opposed to perpendicular to it). Wood does wear over time, even when protected and painted, which can give it a nice weathered look. Metal has the advantage of lasting longer, but it's nonrenewable and more expensive.

Locally available natural materials can also be used. Fences made of willow branches or even dried twigs are both rustic and elegant, although they do eventually degrade and thus require maintenance. Willows have been cultivated for thousands of years for their ability to create flexible fencing material. These fences are more friendly to local flora and fauna by providing a small habitat for moss, lichens, insects, and more.

Traditionally, people used whatever material was at hand for walls: stone, plant matter, and dried mud. Over time, urban cultures started incorporating metal, cement, stucco, and other refined materials. Each material gives its own unique spin to the garden's elements. The ochre stucco typically associated with Tuscany has a warm feeling; the white stucco with blue paint associated with the Greek islands is clean and bright; and the adobe and stone walls of the southwestern US look like extensions of the landscape itself.

Walls and fences can be useful by providing a background to frame a garden's interior. A plant whose predominant color is green will look very different depending on the color and texture of the wall behind it. It's a great way to experiment. Red, blue, or gray backgrounds not only have a unique energy but also make whatever is inside the garden stand out differently.

Living plants make excellent garden boundaries, much like the example of the ocotillo fence. More prolific hedges can be pruned to have a wall-like quality, and European gardens have long used box hedges because of their ability to be sculpted into a variety of shapes. In Europe, farmers have historically planted and maintained hedgerows to keep grazing animals out of the garden. These hedgerows were often composed of multipurpose plants, such as hazelnut, that could be used by people in various ways. We can design hedgerows in our gardens, choosing plants based on how tall we want the barrier to get. Living barriers like these not only create a physical obstacle to enter but also a visual screen, while providing habitat for flora and fauna (birds love the protection that hedgerows provide). They are also cheaper than traditionally built fences and walls.

But a garden doesn't need a fence or a wall or anything to mark where it ends. Although it may be necessary to mark boundaries in some situations, it's important to remember that these boundaries are human inventions, placed onto a planet that is inherently without borders. With this in mind, perhaps we can define our gardens with a bit more humility and playfulness.

OPPOSITE, TOP
A living boundary of California natives, including California poppy (*Eschscholzia californica*), separates the sidewalk from the vegetable garden in Salinas, California.

OPPOSITE, LEFT
We can upset boundaries by turning them into gathering places, like this corner bench in Berkeley, California.

OPPOSITE, RIGHT
An elevated screen in Kensington, California, gives privacy to a home, without separating the garden from the surroundings. The owner said, "I want to walk around naked without my neighbors seeing me."

CHAPTER FOUR

PATHS—TELLING THE STORY

OPPOSITE, TOP
A path follows the contours of the hillside. Wood stumps from a deceased, local oak tree retains the hillside for the path and provides habitat for insects.

OPPOSITE, BOTTOM
Thoughtful paths open us up to the beauty around us, like these stone islands at Los Garambullos, San Miguel de Allende, Mexico.

Paths take us on journeys. By influencing where we move and where we look in the garden, paths affect how we feel. In large gardens—a park, for example—we might move through a variety of spaces, each with its own energy. We may enter from a parking lot or a bus stop and move through a shadowy canopy of trees onto an open, sunny prairie. In smaller gardens, like balcony gardens, our eyes or hands move through the space, studying this flower, rubbing and smelling that leaf. Gardens are not just places. They are experiences through time. In this chapter, we will focus on how paths organize and disorganize garden spaces and thus construct and shape how we experience gardens. As always, my goal is not to prescribe a specific way of gardening or laying out paths, but instead to raise questions that will help each of us make our own decisions.

To begin, paths don't just take us from point A to point B. We tend to follow paths with our eyes to see where they are going. They create a geometry that helps us make sense of a place and curate our attention. The gardens of French and

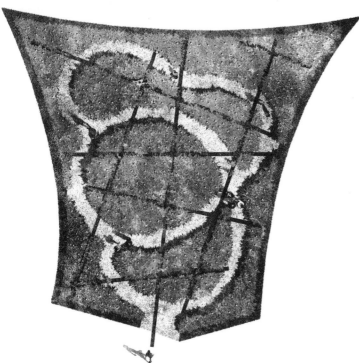

ABOVE
Rectilinear pathways can bring order and legibility to a space, as in this community garden at New Westminster, British Columbia.

LEFT
Two overlapping path systems—one wide and curved, the other linear and narrow—form the structure of Into the Woods and allow visitors to explore by following their instincts.

Italian nobility in the sixteenth and seventeenth centuries tended to be organized around clear geometries such as circles, squares, and straight lines. These gardens were often designed to be seen from a particular vantage point that allowed the visitor to see, and thus understand, the whole garden in one glance.

This classical style of gardening, using simple linear geometries, remains useful today because of how it organizes space in a clear and legible way. Landscape architect Joan Iverson Nassauer coined the phrase "messy ecosystems, orderly frames" to refer to the role that those simple geometries can play in helping people appreciate "messy" nature. Basic shapes, instead of creating harmonious order, can also be used to generate tension, giving an edge. For example, a path can break the symmetry of a garden by crossing it at an angle. Intentional moves like this, however uncomplicated, can feel bold and exciting. In contrast to straight lines, curves feel more natural and organic—perhaps because straight lines are rare in the natural world.

Paths also tell stories because, as they lead us through a garden space, they interact with other elements in the garden, generating a landscape of feelings within us. Let's look at a specific example: Into the Woods was designed for the 2018 International Garden Festival in Chaumont-sur-Loire, France. Inspired by a story by the Argentine author Jorge Luis Borges, the garden was organized around two path layouts. The first and main path consisted of a wider path of decomposed granite that curved through the garden. The second was a network of charred cedar timber that crisscrossed the space at various angles, moving through the trees. Where the timbers met the main path, the designers lowered the timbers, making them flush with the decomposed granite. When a visitor entered the garden, they had an infinite set of options. They could stay on the curved wide path, or hop on to the wood timbers and immerse themselves in the foliage of the trees. Children and playful adults loved this garden because they could actually explore it, instead of having to walk through it in a predictable way. It was a garden full of mystery and possibility.

The planks in the Into the Woods garden allow visitors to move off the main path and into the mystery and intimacy of the tree foliage.

OPPOSITE
Children and playful adults are attracted to the raised plank paths of Into the Woods.

The key to this garden's success was how well the dense plantings screened paths from view. Not knowing where a path goes creates a sense of excitement, curiosity, and apprehension in a visitor. Screening a path, through plants or architecture, is a great strategy for creating a sense of depth and for making a garden feel bigger. Screens can be fully opaque, completely blocking out what is behind, or semitransparent, giving the visitor a little glimpse of what lies beyond.

The storytelling ability of a path has to do with its relationship to the rest of the garden. Does it blend seamlessly into its surrounding, making it almost invisible? Or does it stand out with clear edges of demarcation? How and where do other elements meet the path? Into the Woods had an easy-to-move-through main path, with no obstacles, objects, or branches in the way, but the secondary network of timber paths moved through the tree canopy. On a material level, when the two path systems interacted, the main path had priority, and the planks went flush with it.

A well-defined path guides our experience in a more predictable way. The story it tells is clear and orderly. In contrast, loosely defined paths feel more informal and less ordered. The edges of a path play an important role in how the path relates to the rest of the garden. Is the path lined with a metal divider, with stones, or with little sculptures? Or is it made of gravel that blends into the surrounding vegetation? Allowing vegetation to grow over a path helps integrate the path into the surroundings. On the other hand, paths made of materials that contrast with the rest of the garden will stand out. For example, a gravel path in a garden whose surface is predominantly made of rock and gravel will blend in, but a wooden boardwalk over the same garden will be more visible.

It's not always necessary to design specific paths for a garden. A layout can be planted first, which allows the remaining space to become a place of circulation. Paths can also emerge spontaneously as people and wildlife trample the ground over time (these are known as *desire lines*).

Path making encourages us to ask important questions: How do we want to organize or disorganize the spaces around us? What stories do we want these spaces to share? And what materials will make this possible?

ABOVE
The forest of Into the Woods consists of poplar (*Populus trichocarpa* x *deltoides*), goat willow (*Salix caprea*), hairy birch (*Betula pubescens*), black locust (*Robinia pseudoacacia*), sycamore maple (*Acer pseudoplatanus*), and red alder (*Alnus rubra*).

OPPOSITE, TOP
Where the two path systems overlap in Into the Woods, the planks become flush with the gravel of the main path.

OPPOSITE, BOTTOM
These hexagonal stepping-stones link two garden islands with playfulness and elegance.

CHAPTER FIVE

PAVING AND SURFACES— CRAFTING THE GROUND

OPPOSITE, TOP
A driveway garden in San Francisco proves the point that anything can be a garden.

OPPOSITE, BOTTOM
Permeable pavers filled with creeping mint, and a central strip of succulents and various types of thyme allow rain to seep into the ground. Nothing grows taller than six inches or else it gets nipped by the car.

There is a driveway in San Francisco's Castro neighborhood that is worth noting. It's a fully functioning driveway, used daily, with a median strip of thyme and succulents, and permeable, concrete pavers filled with creeping mint. Nothing gets taller than six inches, or else it gets nipped by a car pulling in.

This driveway takes something practical and conventional— a surface to drive on—and turns it into something more: a garden. If paths take us from one place to another, then paving is how they do that. Unfortunately, our culture gravitates toward what we know best: asphalt and concrete. These do an excellent job of providing smooth surfaces for bikes, cars, and wheelchairs. In some cases, like public spaces, I believe asphalt and concrete are the best solution. However, our ability to get creative with the ground has atrophied. When we start thinking about paths as more than a practical way to get from A to B, a world of possibility opens up. Can paths, roads, and driveways be works of art? Can these lowly things that we step and drive on become gardens? In this chapter, we are going to look at how

paving and surface materials can meet our practical needs for movement, offer endless creative possibilities, and provide habitat for other beings.

Let's start with our practical, day-to-day needs. We humans are mobile creatives. We move around our homes and gardens, and we move through our cities and landscapes. There are good reasons why our cities are so completely paved over. Surface materials, such as bricks, gravel, concrete pavers, and wood, provide surfaces on which to step on so we don't slip and so we don't trample the ground. These surfaces keep our feet and shoes from getting wet and muddy, and provide smooth, long-lasting surfaces for pedestrians, cyclists, and rivers on which to move around.

But the ground doesn't just have to be a surface we use. It can also be a place we honor that can add color and texture to our journeys. A well-constructed stone-paver path is not just useful, it's full of shapes and textures that inspire us. In Japan, for example, the laying of stones for a garden path, which is a symbol for the journey of life, is a sacred task. The art of laying pavers becomes a spiritual task of offering a pleasing journey for all who will use it. So, the practical needs of the path must be balanced with its appearance. The type and size of stone and the spacing between the stones are meticulously worked on and harmonized to achieve a desired effect.

LEFT
The paving at the Portland Japanese Garden makes us appreciate craftsmanship and focuses our attention on the small details of life.

RIGHT
The colors and textures of these stone pavers and gravel complement each other at the Nitobe Memorial Garden, a traditional Japanese stroll garden, at the University of British Columbia Botanical Gardens, Vancouver.

Beyond the practical and the aesthetic, there is another incredibly important aspect of ground surfaces, and that is the habitats they provide for other life forms, especially plants and insects. I love seeing paving systems that allow for plants to grow in the spaces between the pavers. It's easy to forget that the surfaces we step on can be somebody's home. It's important to remember that our needs and those of other species can and must coexist.

By harboring soil and influencing the flow of water, ground surfaces, like pavers, provide different habitats for plants and animals. Impermeable surfaces, including concrete, stone, brick, wood, and asphalt, redirect the flow of rain away from a surface. Because the water has to go *somewhere*, they require some type of drainage infrastructure, such as open drains, retention basins, and ponds outside the surface area. One issue with our current model of urban development is that we use so many impermeable surfaces. Water that used to seep into the ground now gets flushed into the sewer system or into lakes and oceans. On the other hand, permeable surfaces, including decomposed granite, gravel, mulch, grid pavers, GraniteCrete, and certain concretes, have pores and empty spaces that allow water to percolate (flow down) through them to varying degrees. They provide a solid surface to step on while still allowing water to filter into the ground.

Our surface materials also impact the presence of soil. Because impermeable surfaces are smooth, they aren't ideal places for soil and dust to settle and accumulate. Plants tend to grow spontaneously from the cracks of the sidewalks, because the roots of a plant can find the moisture and soil it needs in those cracks. This is why impermeable surfaces don't provide good habitat for plants, unless they have gaps and holes between them. Even tiny gaps of one-sixteenth of an inch will be settled by spontaneous plants. Larger gaps can be opened up in impermeable surfaces to provide space to plant or sow seeds in. The best plants to integrate into paving systems are short and tough, so you can walk on them without worrying, and spread quickly in order to fill the space between pavers.

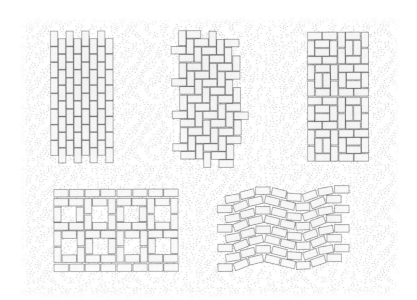

OPPOSITE
Stone cobbles arc gracefully
around a native western
sycamore (*Platanus
racemosa*) in this Southern
Californian courtyard.

RIGHT
Five ways of using sixty-
four bricks.

Creeping thyme and Irish moss are two of the most common
paver fillers in the United States.

Surface materials can still provide habitat for plants and
other species. Rounded wood pavers provide a smooth surface
on which to walk, and they are impermeable. Over time, however, they absorb moisture and can become home for mosses,
lichen, and mushrooms, before eventually decomposing back
into soil. In contrast, gravel does not decompose (during our
life-span at least). A thick layer of gravel will not provide any
habitat for plants at first. Over the years however, dust, soil,
and the seeds of plants will start to accumulate, and you will
see brave species colonizing the space.

Once the practical, aesthetic, and ecological aspects of
surface materials are explored, we can integrate them and consider different strategies. One approach is to use a single material in new and unconventional ways. Bricks and cobblestones
can be arranged in an infinite variety of ways. Alternatively,
two or more paving materials can play off each other. Brick and
tile, flagstone and river rock, decomposed granite and wood,
and pea gravel and cobbles are great combinations. We can
edge one material with the other, create a rhythmic pattern, or
mix them randomly. One of the materials may be a base layer

onto which another material is laid. Flagstones, for example, are often laid in decomposed granite or on gravel.

We are familiar with the classic paver materials. Stone varies in size, shape, and origin, from formal cut stones to irregular flagstones, boulders, cobbles, and river rocks. Bricks, pea gravel, decomposed granite, and precast pavers also come in all shapes and colors. What excites me the most, however, is the wide availability of recycled paving materials and all the creative opportunities they give us. In reality, pretty much anything can be embedded in a paving system, from old metal factory parts to glass bottles and old fence posts. It's not the material that matters—it's the inventive way it is used that will show intention and make a place special.

Pavers may seem unimportant or frivolous parts of a garden, but their practicality, their impact on water and soil, and their creative diversity provide fantastic opportunities for us to think outside the box and challenge expectations. If paths bring us from one place to another, pavers and surface materials make the journey itself enjoyable.

ABOVE
Stained concrete pavers add a touch of whimsy to this garden by California artist Keeyla Meadows.

OPPOSITE, TOP
Old industrial gears, wood cylinders, and gravel work together to compose this garden near Seattle.

OPPOSITE, BOTTOM
Stone pavers, placed askew, give vibrancy to this small, private courtyard-garden in Brooklyn.

CHAPTER SIX

EDGES—DEFINING SPACE

In 2021, Wagon Landscaping, a Paris-based landscape architecture studio, was asked to design a garden in the courtyard of a Parisian apartment complex. The courtyard, however, was covered in asphalt. Undeterred, Wagon's team cut out two hundred square feet of asphalt and loosened the soil and gravel mix that lay underneath. They then mixed fresh soil to the existing soil and gravel, and planted into this new mix. In order to not remove anything from the site, they reused the removed asphalt chunks and placed them vertically, side by side, alongside a wooden edge.

Entitled Asphalt Jungle, this project takes a material that most people consider useless and literally reframes it. Wagon Landscaping avoids removing materials from a site because they believe everyday materials like asphalt are an asset. Such intentions open up possibilities. The granular asphalt is full of texture and contrasts well with the lighter tone of the wood and the green of the plants. The result is an edge that separates the planting area from the surrounding asphalt.

OPPOSITE, LEFT
Wagon Landscaping's Asphalt Jungle converts an asphalt-covered Parisian courtyard into a garden and reuses the decompacted asphalt as edging material.

OPPOSITE, RIGHT
Plants and recycled urban waste coexisting peacefully at Asphalt Jungle.

A metal edging strip subtly separates path from planting area at the Chadwick Arboretum and Learning Gardens at the Ohio State University.

OPPOSITE
One of the functions of edges is to frame. Wood and asphalt at Asphalt Jungle frame the garden like a painting.

An edge, when it comes to paths and garden design, is simply the end of one area and the beginning of another. We can demarcate that edge with something material—and there are good reasons to do this. A separating edge can be functional—helping prevent soil from spilling onto a walking area, for instance. Edges can also serve a purely visual role, by defining the boundary of a path or by creating a threshold that announces the beginning of a new garden space. They can divide a large area into smaller, more intimate spaces. These divisions can be abrupt and clear (i.e., function like walls) or they can be soft (e.g., gravel gradually giving way to soil). Whereas chapter three focuses on the outer boundaries of the garden and what this implies about the garden, here we're broadening our scope to look at how we define any edge at all.

Although edges might seem like minor details in the garden, they are powerful tools that help us define space. We humans respond to shapes and lines because these give us a sense of order and narrative. Although the plantings inside Asphalt Jungle are not orderly, the wood and asphalt edge organize the space. They demonstrate a desire, on the part of Wagon Landscaping, to make the courtyard special and unique. Without that edge, the garden would look less cared for. These details matter. When we look at the asphalt edging of Asphalt Jungle, it's hard not to appreciate its thoughtfulness, and, in that feeling of appreciation, we feel connected to the garden and those who helped make it.

Edges have height. When they are at or near ground level, they serve mainly to separate materials from each other or to mark a specific geometry, such as the shape of a path or the boundary of a planting area. Plastic and metal divider strips are commonly used in residential landscape design. Metal dividers, because of their thinness, are useful in subtly separating ground materials. But the reality is that anything that can be used as paving—bricks, stone, gravel, and recycled objects (e.g., glass bottles, scrap metal)—can also be used for low edges. Wood can be laid horizontally flat on the ground, or vertically. Willow branches are great material for edging because

they grow locally in most parts of the Northern Hemisphere. I have even seen broken teacups used for low edges in gardens!

When edges get taller—rising more than a few inches above the ground—they gain visual prominence and mark off spaces more boldly. This may visually define a space, or it may be more functional, like preventing people or animals from trampling a planting area. Low walls not only help mark off a space but also double up as a seating surface. A series of plants can line the edge of a path, distinguishing the path from its surroundings. When a path crosses an edge, "breaking" through it, it creates the sensation of moving through a threshold. When edges get even higher—taller than a person—the threshold effect is strengthened because it obstructs our vision. An arbor, for example, completely surrounds us: psychologically, it's like passing through a portal. Fences, walls, screens, and trees can likewise be used to create portals into garden rooms.

There is a garden on Vine Street in Berkeley, California, with a particularly impressive "portal." Where the garden meets the sidewalk, the owners have placed a doorframe and its door. Wisteria and flowering jasmine grow along and above the door frame, which acts like an arbor of sorts. I love this example because it really gives the feeling of entering a garden *room*. The door serves no purpose from a purely practical

A GARDEN'S PURPOSE

BELOW
Concrete has a terrible carbon footprint, but these hand-cast concrete columns form an elegant, variable edge. Use recycled concrete when you can!

standpoint—it's not locked and you can just walk around it into the garden. Its purpose is to create a threshold that playfully and lightheartedly invites us to enter.

At Land's End in San Francisco, Surfacedesign, a local landscape architecture studio, imagined a different type of edge. Amid the native plantings of monkey flower, sagebrush, and coyote brush, the designers planted a series of wooden posts. Arranged in lines, the posts extend from the architecture of the nearby visitor's center. They are actually reclaimed fence posts that serve as dune screens, helping stabilize the sand into which they are planted. The lines of wooden fence posts flow through the landscape and create a series of semitransparent edges. They aren't lining a path or marking off planting areas. They define clear geometries that provide visual order amid the disorder of the native plants.

Edges provide clarity and definition in a garden, but this doesn't mean they are always necessary. Not all paths or plantings need a clear separation from what's around them. In fact, avoiding edges altogether can help unify garden spaces, creating a common ground material for, say, planting areas and patio spaces. It's also possible to have gradual, or "soft" edges, in which the transition between two garden spaces is spread out over a distance, such as a sandy garden area gradually giving way to a gravel area. The transition space between two different materials becomes an interesting area in and of itself. And edges are ways of highlighting contrast. This can be seen in the simple act of mowing grass: the path left behind by the lawnmower highlights the contrast between tall grass and short stubble. Edges help us appreciate difference. When used well, they create spaces that celebrate the diversity of shapes, colors, and materials in our world.

OPPOSITE, TOP
Repurposed wooden posts frame the plantings of coast buckwheat (*Eriogonum latifolium*), California sagebrush (*Artemisia californica*), orange bush monkeyflower (*Diplacus aurantiacus*), and coyote brush (*Baccharis pilularis*) at Land's End in San Francisco.

OPPOSITE, BOTTOM
A ground material without edges can help unify living and planted spaces.

CHAPTER SEVEN

SLOPES—STEPPING UP AND DOWN

The mountains of the northern Philippines are home to one of the world's most unique landscapes. The local Ifugao ethnic group have used stone to terrace entire mountainsides to create flat surfaces for rice farming. An intricate irrigation system harvests water from forests uphill and spreads them through the rice paddies. Although unique, the Philippines rice terraces are not alone. Across the world, in mountainous and hilly areas, people have created and continue to create terraces to provide level land for farming and living.

We don't live in a flat world. Regardless of where we live, we constantly experience small and big changes in elevation. These variations may be minor, like sidewalk curbs or stairs, or they may be major, like hills or high-rises. We are so used to these changes that we often forget how they impact our day-to-day life. Slopes can be challenging to walk up or down because horizontal surfaces are what give us the grip we need to step forward as we walk. When we walk up a slope or when we are at the bottom of a set of steps, we look up and orient ourselves

OPPOSITE, TOP
Concrete, wood, and vegetation form the basis of a residential retaining system in Berkeley, California. Could this have been done without concrete? Yes!

OPPOSITE, BOTTOM
Even small changes in elevation, like this wooden bridge and seat, add dynamism to a space by engaging our eyes and our bodies.

toward the sky. Coming down the other way, we look down, or into the distance. From heights, we see more, and we can feel empowered and inspired. In traditional cultures the world over, the tops of hills and mountains are often considered sacred, places to be deeply respected.

Slopes have unique environmental conditions that impact our experience of them. Slopes erode more easily than flat areas, making it harder to grow crops. Erosion on slopes also means that rich soil tends to end up at the bottom of valleys instead of the top. Water in the soil of sloped terrains drains downhill. Plants that thrive in well-draining soil prefer slopes, whereas those that thrive in more consistent moisture will prefer the bottom of slopes. In the Northern Hemisphere, southern-facing slopes receive more sunlight than adjacent flat areas, so we often find different plants growing on the northern and southern sides of hills and mountains.

It's important to work imaginatively with topography (the three-dimensional surface of the ground), instead of against it. In our gardens, we can both adapt to existing topography, and create new ones. In flat spaces, mounds and berms are powerful tools to add dynamism and movement. By screening our vision, they also add depth to a landscape, and by blocking sound, they can create quieter, intimate spaces. They can also be used to direct the flow of water toward retention basins or swales.

For all the things slopes do for us, our lives are more convenient on level surfaces, and the most common way to create these around the world is by building a retaining wall. In urban areas the world over, concrete has increasingly become the norm for retaining walls, whether poured in place or via cinder blocks. Concrete is cheap, it can be molded into clear, neat shapes, and it does an excellent job stabilizing slopes; however—and I will repeat this throughout the book—its environmental cost is staggering and its easy availability prevents us from pursuing more creative solutions. Recycled materials, from recycled concrete to car tires, can offer surprisingly elegant solutions to those who actually try them.

On slopes that don't require a retaining wall but that do need some stabilization, plant roots provide an excellent option. Unlike stone, concrete, and other recycled materials, plants are alive. Their roots literally hold the soil together. In recently disturbed sites—such as on slopes that have suffered wildfire, or on badly eroded hillsides—an erosion-control seed mix of annual plants, available at most local nurseries, can be sown to create a rapid network of plant roots to hold the soil. Where time is less of an issue, perennial plants can be used; their roots will grow over the years. Biodegradable materials can also be used in conjunction with seed mixes and perennials to stabilize slopes. Jute netting laid on slopes will prevent water erosion, protect seed mixes from rain, wind, and sun, and biodegrade over time. Branches can also be laid along contour lines (perpendicular to the slope) to create micro-terraces.

In addition to stabilizing slopes and creating flat spaces on them, we also need to move up and down slopes, and the single greatest technology for achieving this is the step. Look around any garden, even the flattest ones, and you will notice a step somewhere. But the design of steps is a little-discussed art form with tremendous room for play and exploration.

ABOVE
Woody vegetation on a site can be used to create micro retaining walls, as seen here at Blake Garden in Kensington, California.

OPPOSITE
The metal stairs of this home in Ubatuba, Brazil, allow us to see through to the ground below, giving the impression that the stairs float above the slope.

OPPOSITE, TOP
Four ways of going up five
feet. Clockwise from top right:
tight treads facing slope, thin
treads facing slope with filler,
spaced-out treads facing
slope, treads perpendicular
to slope with a retaining wall.

OPPOSITE, BOTTOM
Retaining walls can have
multiple functions, here
serving as a chalkboard
and a bouldering surface.

Steps can run directly up and down a slope or perpendicular to it. Each creates different sighting opportunities. Running up and down, steps lead the eye up to the sky or down toward the ground. Perpendicular to the slope, we are face to face with the angle of the slope, with the upslope on one side and the downslope on the other.

The geometry of steps also creates different effects. The tread of a step is the horizontal spacing between steps, and the riser is the vertical difference between them. Big treads and small risers decrease the angle that the user has to go up or down, creating a less strenuous and more spacious experience. Wide treads are also excellent platforms for pots and artwork. In smaller gardens or on steep slopes, there may be no choice but to have steep steps.

The steps themselves can be made of a single material (e.g., concrete, stone pavers, recycled tires), or a combination of materials. Materials naturally existing onsite—such as stone and wood—will usually blend in better, although they can be arranged in different ways. Stone pavers, for example, can be spaced out like stepping-stones on a slope, or grouped together to create a larger tread. Plants, rocks, artwork, and other materials can create an edge to the stairs, helping integrate them into the slope or, conversely, helping them stick out. The same rules that apply for paths also apply to steps: the choice of materials will impact whether the steps will blend into the space or jump out. Are the materials used for the steps used anywhere else in the garden? What natural and locally available materials—from stone to wood stumps—can be integrated into the design?

Steps, retaining walls, and soil stabilization strategies are all practical ways of designing on slopes. However, slopes are amazing places in and of themselves—we don't always have to "do" things to them. They catch the light in different ways than flat places do, and often attract unique plants and animals. The practical challenges of walking, sitting, and standing on slopes make these areas engaging to interact with. Children, for example, love steep slopes because adults are usually not there.

OPPOSITE
Slopes aren't just challenging sites to "deal" with; they offer unique conditions that are interesting in and of themselves.

RIGHT
Stairs aren't the only way up and down. The challenges posed by slopes can be embraced as opportunities to think creatively, as with this slope-side garden by Terremoto.

It's worth asking ourselves: How much do we really want to modify a slope? What's the least we can do with greatest impact? And, conversely, if we are in a flat space, what simple interventions—like a raised paver—can change our awareness of the space? The goal of this book, as always, is not to prescribe a specific way of gardening or designing but to instill wonder in the world around us. Gravity is real. Experimenting with topography—with stairs, slopes, and retaining walls—is a playful way to reexamine a place.

CHAPTER EIGHT

POTS, PLANTERS, AND OTHER CONTAINERS— CARRYING THE GARDEN

OPPOSITE
Containers help us appreciate the beauty of plants by framing them. Here, a blue plumbago (*Plumbago auriculata*) in a terra-cotta pot transforms the energy of a space.

Of all the objects and things in a garden, pots, planters, and containers might just win the popularity award. They are everywhere: in our patios, streets, balconies, and on our desks and in our hallways. Look around you right now, and there's a good chance you'll find a plant-bearing container within eye-sight. They hover over our beds and sofas, peek at us through the shower curtain, and cheer us on throughout the day. They allow plants to thrive in all types of spaces where they previously couldn't: where there is no soil, where the soil is poor, in tight narrow spaces, and indoors. For those who rent homes, containers are a way to bring plants easily into our space. They bring much needed vegetation in urban areas that are covered with asphalt and concrete. Some gardens—such as the Princess Gardens in Berlin (see page 159)—never plant directly into the ground and instead rely entirely on movable containers, either because they don't have access to soil in the ground or because that soil is contaminated. In short, containers are popular because they enable us to extend our

gardens and integrate vegetation more closely into all aspects of our lives.

Containers (here understood as any device that contains soil for plants) do something very simple: they hold soil in place. I'm amazed by how impactful it is to raise the ground level by one or two feet, whether that's in a bigger planter or a single pot: it allows us to get that much closer to the beautiful action of plant growth, without having to bend over or get on our knees. These changes also greatly increase the accessibility of gardens, by allowing those that have limited or compromised mobility to work the soil with greater ease. Containers are also easy to control: we can water them when we want and move them to new locations. And whether it's one fern in a ceramic pot, or lettuce, carrots, and beets in a planter, they frame plants visually and thus honor them as the living beings they are.

Designing with containers involves understanding them as mini-ecosystems, where heat, light, moisture, and the container material interact. In a garden, moisture in a given

Containers allow us to extend the garden to all parts of our lives, from our homes to our streets and offices.

Recycled metal cans repurposed as small containers form the backbone of this garden at the International Garden Festival of Chaumont-sur-Loire.

volume of soil diffuses to the surrounding soil. The soil in a container, however, is disconnected from the ground, which cannot provide it with additional moisture. Heat and sunlight will dry the soil in containers faster than the surrounding soil. It's why small balcony containers tend to dry up so quickly. This is neither good nor bad; it's only something to be aware of.

Drainage holes at the bottom or the sides of a container influence how much moisture the container retains, determining what plants will thrive in it. Plants native to arid regions will appreciate a container that drains readily, whereas vegetables enjoy a more consistent moisture. I love to grow arid-climate succulents (such as agaves) in well-draining containers; even if it rains, the drainage holes allow excess water to flow out. Planters, whose soil is connected to native soil beneath them,

OPPOSITE, TOP
The ferns in hanging containers in New Orleans benefit from the stable humidity in the air.

OPPOSITE, BOTTOM
The washed-out, earthy tones of terra-cotta pots contrast with the green tones of the surrounding vegetation.

will retain moisture more readily, as water moves up by capillary action from the soil underneath and into the planter. It's also possible to not have any drainage holes. Watertight containers (e.g., small bowls, large galvanized stock tanks) can be used to create bog gardens (with plants that flourish in wet soil but without their roots completely submerged) or water gardens (with plants that thrive with their roots completely submerged).

The material of a container is important not only for its appearance but also how it impacts the soil inside. Terra-cotta pots are made of baked clay that absorbs moisture and releases it slowly over time to the soil inside. Terra-cotta pots are also thicker than the plastic pots one finds in nurseries. This thicker layer insulates the soil from the sun's rays. Metal doesn't provide great insulation, but can offer a distinctive look. For example, Corten planters offer clean edges with an earthy tone while corrugated sheet metal feels more industrial.

One of the greatest advantages of using containers is the ability to experiment. Coming back from a nursery, we can leave a pot in a particular place and see how the plant does. We can leave it there or move it to somewhere with different conditions. Using containers is a great, noncommittal way to place plants in new and experimental spots. And for those living in cold-weather climates, containers allow us to move our plants inside during the winter and outside during the summer.

Containers don't just hold soil and plants. They can be beautiful objects unto themselves. They can imbue a space with a distinctive feeling. Looking at the garden on pages 92 and 93 we can see how the planters create narrow corridors and wider gathering spaces. The spaces in between the planters have a sunken quality to them, almost as if one were starting to walk underground. The color and texture of the Corten metal also has an earthy quality that looks a lot like soil, and contrasts well with the lighter decomposed granite.

A container's visual effect depends on its context. Does the material or color of the container find resonance in other parts of the garden? Should the container blend into the

surroundings, or should it be painted in bright colors so that it stands out? A simple strategy to brighten up a garden is to paint planters in colors that contrast those of the garden.

The arrangement and choice of containers create vastly different effects. By itself in a prominent location, a pot can be a real work of art. Arranged in a line, identical containers can look orderly, whereas different containers arranged in a line will feel more informal. Stairs and corners make great locations for containers: placing a pot on each tread creates a cascading effect, and tight corner spaces can be softened up with a container. Containers can also be hung on vertical surfaces, either directly on walls, or through the use of shelves.

The great news is that almost anything can be a container or can be used to create one. Urban recycling centers are fantastic places to look for both conventional and unconventional materials for containers. Bathtubs, fountains, even old toilets

ABOVE
Containers don't have to be secondary elements in a garden. Here, the shapes of the containers structure the space.

OPPOSITE
Elevating the ground via containers brings plants closer to eye level. Here, the shape of the Corten containers gives a clean, edgy feeling to the space.

OPPOSITE, TOP
Many recycled materials make
excellent containers, like
these repurposed terra-cotta
flue liners in Seattle.

OPPOSITE, BOTTOM
Painting containers in
contrasting hues brings
unexpected brightness to the
Majorelle Garden in Marrakesh.

can serve as planters. Or if these suggestions horrify you and you want a cleaner feel, look for metal drums, clay flue liners, and sections of wide metal pipes. The possibilities are endless. Note that if edible plants are being used, the material must not have been treated with chemicals, as is generally the case with pressure-treated wood and railroad ties.

Containers allow us to expand the garden to include all parts of our lives. The plants they host enrich our lives and provide a special kind of companionship. Now I have a confession: I have a huge *Monstera deliciosa*, or Swiss cheese plant, in a pot next to my bed. Its leaves reach out and extend over the bed. When I toss and turn at night, its leaves caress me back to sleep. Containers and their relatives make sure the garden is always within arm's or leaf's reach, and their inhabitants always close.

CHAPTER NINE

REST AND PLAY—UNWINDING WITH THE GARDEN

San Francisco–based landscape architect Anooshey Rahim likes simple interventions with big impact. On the sloped backyard of one of her residential projects, she connected four stumps of eucalyptus wood with posts, creating a structure that looks like a combination balance beam, bench, and sculpture. Designed as a play structure for the client's children, its natural form and unusual shape invite all to play with it in whatever way feels appropriate. It's a straightforward intervention, made with everyday materials that anyone with basic tools and the desire could make. This simplicity, Rahim says, is meant to show that "cool design can be uncomplicated."

Rahim's design is playful because it encourages us to enjoy the garden in an open-ended way, without specific goals. It reminds us of the importance of being playful with our gardens. Why is the world of garden design so serious? Maybe we've been looking at gardens in the same way for too long. Cultivating a playful attitude means looking at the world around us with fresh, childlike eyes and exploring new ways of imagining a space or using an object.

OPPOSITE
Four eucalyptus stumps and three crossbeams create an open-ended play structure. The designer, Anooshey Rahim of Dune Hai, wants to show "cool design can be uncomplicated."

LEFT
A simple wooden platform sits at an angle, atop a fallen tree trunk, for visitors to admire the Ika Stream and its surroundings.

BELOW
From afar, the Ika Stream platform appears completely immersed in the forest.

For example, in the forests of Transylvania (in northwestern Romania), Studio Nomad, in collaboration with Batlab, crafted a meditation platform on a collapsed bank of the Ika Stream. Designed to invite visitors to look at their surroundings with awareness, the platform is basic: it's a twelve-foot-wide wooden disc, secured onto a fallen tree, supported by wooden columns buried in the ground. The angle of the fallen tree gives the platform a slight downhill incline, orienting viewers toward the stream. The designers used the fallen tree as a support because they didn't want the platform to appear too contrived. They wanted visitors to appreciate their surroundings and not focus on the platform. From afar, the disc appears to float, immersed in the forest, like an extraterrestrial object.

The Ika Stream platform is a great example of using basic geometries to define a space that invites us to pause, relax, and rest. If play means looking around us with fresh eyes, then rest means taking the time to appreciate where we are, both physically and emotionally. Rest means slowing down and turning our attention not just to where we are, but also to how we are and to all that we carry within us. It means nurturing our connection with nature and remembering that we are part of nature, not apart from it. We live in a predominantly materialist culture that pressures us to be constantly productive. This approach to living can stifle creativity, dull the senses, and corrode our individual and collective welfare. Rest and play are *vital* to our well-being. It's so easy to forget this. Rest and play in the garden foster connection with ourselves, with others, and with place.

A lot of creative possibilities emerge when we start thinking of the garden in terms of rest and play. Patios, decks, benches, pergolas, and fireplaces are classic and powerful ways of creating restful spaces in the garden. Yet these interventions often fail when they detract from the existing beauty of the space. When planning a rest or play area, we can ask ourselves: What's the least we can do with the maximum effect? Do we really need another concrete seating element? What can help us better appreciate our surroundings? Instead of intense, heavy changes on the land, it's more interesting to look at minimalist, elegant interventions that sit lightly on it and encourage us to marvel.

Some changes are amazingly simple, like placing a chair in a meadow. Hay bales make excellent surfaces for sitting, lying, and building—and hay will eventually biodegrade to feed the soil. Rustic benches can be made of locally cut tree trunks and fallen wood. When the weather is nice, we can even place old carpets on the ground to create an outdoor living room. And let's not forget the power of fabric! A garden designed by Los Angeles–based landscape studio Terremoto uses white fabric overhead as a shade screen during the day. At night, the fabric can be dropped vertically to frame the night sky. Simple, versatile, powerful.

ABOVE
Slope, wooden play structure, and vegetation all working in harmony at one of Terremoto's gardens.

RIGHT
Nets and ropes attached to the wooden play structure add opportunities for risk-taking and play.

Chapter Nine: Rest and Play—Unwinding with the Garden

As in the Ika Stream project, simply creating a level surface in uneven places, or framing an area with posts, or even mowing a corner of lawn, can give significance to a place and invite others to appreciate it. Alternatively, creating obstacles and making a space more complex and challenging invites us to engage and play with the space. For example, Terremoto created a playground on the slope of a residential backyard, complete with a slide, wood stumps, swing, nets, and a climbable wooden play structure, all seamlessly integrated into the hillside. The obstacles here become opportunities. Instead of flattening a slope in the name of convenience, we can think of roughing them up, creating barriers that encourage creative problem solving.

One interesting approach is to ask whether a rest or play space looks inward or outward. Inward-looking spaces are usually enclosed and protected from the outside by planting or screens. They may have a central element, such as a water feature, and peripheral elements like benches. These spaces focus our attention on a contained area, providing an opportunity for introspection and meditation. Others may prefer outward-looking spaces. These have views of the surroundings and give us that expansive feeling we get when we look at a landscape from above.

We can combine the best of both worlds by creating a rest space that looks out at the world from a protected nook. Places that provide people with the capacity to see in the distance without being seen often make us feel safe and secure. This observation is known as "prospect-refuge theory" and is usually explained by the fact that being hidden (refuge) while able to spot danger (prospect) held an evolutionary advantage for humans; in short, we feel safe in such spaces. This theory can inspire us to frame views of our surroundings or build tree houses and raised decks tucked within vegetation. Terremoto's deck at Museum Way in Los Angeles (see page 99) offers views to the surrounding, while the fabric gives refuge, screening from the elements and the gaze of others.

A GARDEN'S PURPOSE

Thinking creatively about our rest and play spaces invite us to relate to our surroundings in new and unexpected ways. For example, in the Cévennes mountain range in the south of France, designer Amaury Poudray created a raised wooden platform with a sunken area to lie down in. The wood paneling in the sunken area is angled to provide a comfortable position to look at the night sky. It would have been easier for Poudray to design a flat platform. His elegant innovation—crafting an angled, protected nook—turns what would otherwise be a regular deck into a stargazing platform. It invites us to relate differently to our surroundings.

We have unlimited capacity to craft spaces for rest, play, and connection—whether it's throwing a bunch of blankets underneath a tree, installing a fountain, or building a sculpture. But rest and play are not just activities we do in the garden; they are also *how* we garden. Gardening is inherently restful and playful; these are two sides of the same coin. Restful because connection to our surroundings recharges us. Playful because that recharge is also a creative boost, helping us admire our world and imagine old things in new ways.

PART THREE

HABITAT

CHAPTER TEN

MAINTENANCE—THE ART OF OBSERVATION

OPPOSITE, TOP
Low-maintenance native prairie instead of green lawn? Yes, says Benjamin Vogt at his home in Lincoln, Nebraska.

OPPOSITE, BOTTOM
From above, Benjamin Vogt's garden contrasts sharply with those of his neighbors.

You can immediately tell which yard belongs to Benjamin Vogt. At the edge of Lincoln, Nebraska, in a suburban development where almost everybody has a flat, green lawn from door to sidewalk, his place sticks out like a sore thumb. The front yard is a bit of wild midwestern prairie plopped down into the heart of suburbia. His quarter acre lot only has a few hundred feet of lawn remaining; everything else is native plants grouped into plant communities that mimic the local native prairie. Short plants with fun names like pale purple coneflower, rattlesnake master, little bluestem, prairie alumroot, and stiff goldenrod share the space with small trees like burr oak and chokecherry. The backyard is even more untamed and connects to a larger wooded area on the edge of the suburban development that acts as a wildlife corridor and bird flyway. Viewed from above, the contrast between Vogt's property and that of his neighbors is stark: a splash of colorful wildness in an ocean of green lawn.

Vogt is a landscape designer with a passion for the native prairie plants of his region, but what is interesting about his

OPPOSITE, LEFT
Benjamin Vogt's time in his garden focuses more on observing and cataloging plant and wildlife activity than traditional maintenance tasks.

OPPOSITE, RIGHT
A patch of mown lawn in the front yard serves as both a pathway and signal to neighbors that this is a looked after space.

OPPOSITE, BELOW
Grasses and dried seed heads catch the early morning frost in Benjamin Vogt's Nebraskan prairie garden.

garden is not what he plants, but how he manages it, or rather how he doesn't manage it. His neighbors mow their lawns once a week during warm weather. Vogt, on the other hand, spends about one day *per year* doing the majority of his garden work, and doesn't provide any irrigation. As he explains it, "With tight-knit plant communities (layers of plants on twelve-inch centers or closer), my big job is cataloging wildlife and observing plant growth—with the occasional yanking of a tree seedling, musk thistle, or bush honeysuckle." Vogt's garden requires little maintenance because the native plants he uses are adapted to the area; they don't need extra irrigation or fertilizer, only an annual cutting back.

If Vogt dedicates time to observing his garden, it's because time spent observing allows him to actually understand the processes of change in his garden. Sometimes, change in a garden is slow and subtle, like grass density decreasing underneath the shade of a growing tree, or lichen slowly colonizing the surface of a rock. Other changes are faster: a storm knocks down branches, a gopher digs a hole into the ground. And some changes last just an instant: the light of the setting sun, piercing through clouds, shedding light on a garden bed. Because gardens are always changing, constantly in progress, our goal is not to avoid change, but to work with it. This is the role of garden management.

We can broaden our understanding of garden management by asking the right questions: What are our goals in the garden? Is it to maintain the legibility of a planting? To promote insect biodiversity? To harvest useful crops? Each goal implies a certain type of management.

For some, the goal is to keep the garden looking the same as always. Everything is pruned and weeded so that no change is apparent. This is the photographic model of garden management. For others, the goal aims for fluidity and spontaneity: allowing volunteer plants to grow, leaving a fallen branch on the ground, or letting a plant go to seed instead of cutting it back. In this approach, the gardener relinquishes some control, and instead cocreates with the garden. Instead of speaking of garden maintenance, which implies stasis, I prefer the term "garden management," which is more open-ended and organic.

Another variable is how much time and effort we want to spend in the garden. High maintenance gardens need constant intervention on the part of the gardener. Some plants not adapted to the climate may need extra water or protection from insects; a green lawn needs to be cut frequently in order to stay short and compact. In contrast, plants adapted to place don't need as many inputs and care. Oftentimes, low-maintenance gardens don't require as much care because they are self-sustaining systems: the various species of plants, wildlife, and fungi work together to balance each other so that no one takes over. For example, providing many different plant habitats in a garden invites diverse insect populations. That insect diversity, in turn, keeps any one insect species from taking over.

Not all parts of the garden need to be managed the same way. We can pick and choose where we spend our time. Some parts of a garden may inherently need more management. Areas with deep, fertile soils, such as rain gardens, will attract opportunistic species that may need cutting back. Other parts of the garden may be out of sight or harder to reach.

There are many strategies available to us in garden management: cutting back, mowing, weeding, burning, pruning, watering, fertilizing, planting, and mulching are just some examples. The most important strategy, however, is observation. There is no point in intervening in a garden that we are not familiar with. In order to see how plants and wildlife live in a garden and how different management strategies impact them, we have to take the time to actually observe. Rebecca McMackin, director of horticulture at the eighty-five-acre Brooklyn Bridge Park in New York City, says that "gardening is not so much about following rules as it is about following rules of observation." McMackin decided to question conventional management strategies by cutting plants back in the spring, and planting in the fall. "Before you act" she claims, "you should question why a task is necessary, and if you really need to do it at all." Terremoto started a project, titled Test

Terremoto's Test Plot is a series of experimental circular gardens, dedicated to monitoring the growth and evolution of California native plants in downtown Los Angeles.

A GARDEN'S PURPOSE

LEFT
A simple sign, and two cute children, let us know that Test Plot is an active research site.

RIGHT
The difference between managed (left) and unmanaged (right) plots in Test Plot demonstrate the impact of active management on the land.

Plot, entirely dedicated to observation-based management. It consists of a series of circular garden plants, each thirty feet in diameter, surrounded by low-budget dune fencing, in central Los Angeles. Terremoto and a team of volunteers watered the soil to promote the growth of weeds and then removed the weeds before they flowered and went to seed. They did this three times in order to weaken the seed bank in the soil. Only then did they plant species native to Southern California, including datura, coyote brush, and buckwheat.

Volunteers from the community care for the plots by planting, watering, thinning, adding mulch, deadheading, and collecting seeds. Test Plot is quite high maintenance, not because the plants need considerable care, but because the goal is meticulous observation. The volunteers catalog the plots via photographs and drawings, noting how the garden changes over time. With its simple circle layout (which is just the radial spray of the small metal spray irrigator they use), Test Plot demonstrates the essence of what a garden is: a living space demarcated from its surroundings with a specific intention in mind.

Many people perceive the wild look of low-maintenance gardens as disorderly and chaotic. To help make these gardens more appealing to the wider public, Benjamin Vogt (with whom we opened the chapter) suggests using a sign with a statement, such as, "This is a low-maintenance, plant pollinator garden." Basic hardscape features, such as sculptures, benches, and trellises can also be incorporated to demonstrate that the garden is not an abandoned piece of land, but an intentional, inhabited space. Vogt also suggests talking to neighbors: "Tell them what you're doing. Invite them over for drinks. Knock on doors and calmly, warmly ask if they'd like to talk about it or see it."

We all have a lot of preconceived ideas about what a garden should look like and how it should be managed. There is—in fact—no single way. The best thing we can do is to observe, act with humility and generosity, and let nature do the rest.

CHAPTER ELEVEN

PLANTS— SIZE AND SHAPE

The graceful twists of the American elm trees (*Ulmus americana*) give a vault-like quality to the Central Park Mall, here during a 2017 snowstorm. Design by Frederick Law Olmsted, Calvert Vaux, and the maintenance team at the Central Park Conservancy.

The Central Park Mall is a fifteen-hundred-foot-long pedestrian esplanade at the heart of Central Park in New York City. Benches, lampposts, and more than 250 American elms, tall and majestic, line the length of this pedestrian avenue. The elms were planted in regular rows in the 1860s. Central Park's designers—Frederick Olmsted and Calvert Vaux—chose these trees because of their graceful, twisting mature branches. They wanted to give the sense that one was entering a grand public room. And they were successful; today the Mall's elm canopy looks like the vaults of a cathedral.

That cathedral-like quality demonstrates the power that plants have on us. Regardless of where we are—the redwood forests of the Pacific Northwest, the windswept prairies of the Midwest, or the bayous of the Mississippi Delta—plants add color to our lives, feed us, provide shelter, and inspire us. And they are alive. Buildings don't change significantly over time, but plants evolve, and so do gardens. Through learning about plants we can see how big an impact they have on us.

Size and shape are a great place to start because they are the easiest to visualize. Everyone knows that plants grow and reach a mature size over time. We use categories like trees, shrubs, and groundcovers to describe the mature size of plants, and these are essentially ways to compare plants to us: when they are mature, some plants grow taller than us, some grow about our size, and others stay close to the ground.

We also know that, beyond size, plants are shaped differently. The foliage of a tree may be rounded like a lollipop, wide and spreading, or narrow like a column. The foliage may hug the ground, or it might start higher up, revealing the trunk. Shrubs can be rounded or asymmetrical. The branching

The native vegetation in this planting design by doxiadis+ in Greece stays close to the ground, giving an open quality to the space.

Plants come in all shapes and sizes. How we design with them impacts the qualities of a space.

structure of plants also varies considerably: the elms of Central Park have twisting branches and a large central trunk, but the Cornelian cherry in other parts of the park are multi-stemmed, appearing to have many small trunks.

One way to understand the impact of plants on our visual field is to imagine plants as creating "garden rooms": plants below the level of the eye compose the floor, those that screen our view are the walls, and the canopy overhead are the ceiling. It sounds silly, but understanding plants this way allows us to design with plants in three dimensions. Rooms can be small and intimate, or large and spacious, like the Mall in Central Park. A garden space may have a floor, but no walls—think of a meadow for example.

The ability of plants to screen and frame our view is of particular importance. Plants, in particular trunks, branches, and shrubs, can be used to frame perspectives in the same way that a frame highlights a painting. A planting area composed of low and medium-sized shrubs is open; standing, we can see beyond it into the distance. However, surrounded by trees and shrubs, our attention is focused nearer; the screen makes what's in the distance feel more distant. In this way, plant screens can add depth to a garden. By redirecting our attention closer to us, they can make a small space feel much larger.

These observations are simple but highly effective. For example, a garden path lined with tall plantings gives the sensation of being immersed in vegetation, whereas a path lined with low plantings that increase in height farther away creates a more spacious feeling, more like walking in a broad valley than in a canyon.

Repetition and creating patterns are powerful tools to give order and structure to a space, or to help accentuate certain geometries. The elms that line the Mall are planted in rows, as are orchards and many agricultural crops. But there is also nothing wrong with planting in a more informal, spontaneous way. "Cramscaping"—planting many plants in a small space without an overarching design scheme—is a perfectly valid strategy; and it's certainly fun.

So far, we have been mainly considering plants on the horizontal plane. For example, when we discussed lining a path with low plantings that increase in height farther away, we were talking about distributing plants either closer or farther away from the path; this is the horizontal plane. But we can

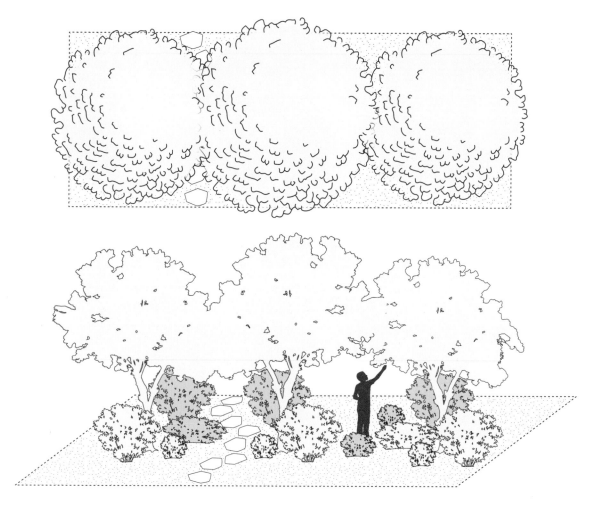

OPPOSITE, TOP
Focusing on the horizontal
plane can hide all the vertical
space that exists beneath
and above plants.

OPPOSITE, BOTTOM
Big plants start small. The
elm trees in this photo of
the Central Park Mall in 1865
are the same as those in the
opening photo of the chapter.

also space plants in the vertical plane. Plants can grow above and below each other. Trees with a narrow trunk and an elevated canopy have significant empty space at their feet. Forests around the world show us how tall trees can shelter smaller plants. These plants, in turn, can shelter even smaller plants, mosses, and lichen. Whether we want to fill that space with as many plants as possible is something we'll discuss in chapter thirteen.

Typically, in an unmanaged piece of land, the tallest plants will be those that need the most light; they grow tall because height is the best way to avoid shade. In contrast, shade-loving plants, like ferns, stay in the shade by staying short relative to their sun-loving neighbors. Even meadows and prairies—which look like they are composed of plants of roughly the same height—typically have multiple vertical layers of plants, adapted to the unique light conditions at a specific moment in time. We can use these basic observations to intentionally plant smaller shade-lovers under the protection of taller sun-lovers.

Up until this point, we have mainly been discussing plants as if they did not grow and change over time. The reality, of course, is that plants are alive; they change considerably over the course of their lifetime. Oaks and Japanese maples grow slowly (less than a foot per year), while eucalyptus, poplars, and willows are known for their rapid growth rate. Deciduous trees lose their leaves during the winter, whereas evergreen trees lose their leaves continuously throughout the year. And plants, like people, get sick, heal, and can die prematurely. Branches fall and new ones grow. The American elms at the Central Park Mall may look static, but they are actually heavily monitored by park management for Dutch elm disease and receive regular treatments of fungicide in order to keep that cathedral-like quality.

So yes, plants can create unique spaces, but they do so over time, in both predictable and unpredictable ways. When designing a garden space, we can use a plant's approximate rate of growth and its mature size to imagine how the space will look in one, five, ten, or fifty years. If planting multiple trees, how will these trees interact over time? Will their canopies merge to create one large roof? Will that canopy create shade in a part of the garden, such as a patio that we prefer to stay sunny?

We can use our knowledge of how plants change seasonally and over the course of their lifetime to optimize elements such as sunlight. For example, homeowners who want sunlight to reach their windows during the winter but prefer shade during summer will want to plant deciduous trees near their homes. Gardeners with limited space who want sunny gardens will want to place trees on the northern side of the garden. In the Northern Hemisphere, shadows are predominantly in the north.

It's impossible to fully predict how plants will grow, but we can make intelligent assumptions to help us create the spaces we want. We also have a variety of maintenance practices to influence how plants grow—which we will discuss more in chapter thirteen. Intelligent planting choices and active garden maintenance work make a good team.

Looking at gardens and all the changes that happen in them, we might ask: Is it us or the plants who are in control? Perhaps it's more like a dance, creating harmony by observing and interacting—human and plant, together.

Plants help "sculpt" space
as with these organ pipe cacti
at Oaxaca's Ethnobotanical
Garden in Mexico.

CHAPTER TWELVE

PLANTS—
COLOR AND TEXTURE

A special surprise awaited visitors to the main stadium at the 2012 Olympic Games in London. Pedestrian routes from the car parks and rail stations to the Olympic Stadium were lined by more than half a mile of flowering meadows. The bloom of one particular meadow, the Olympic Gold Meadows, started orange and blue early in the summer and transformed as the days lengthened to gold and yellow. Visitors were awed by the ocean of color formed by millions of small flower heads—so much so that designated zones had to be set up for people to take their photos with the flowers. One of the main goals of the designers of these meadows, Nigel Dunnett and James Hitchmough, was to touch and inspire people with the power and beauty of the natural world. Most of the public at the Olympic Games had never seen such a vibrant botanical display—and it's safe to say they won't forget the experience.

If the success of the Olympic Gold Meadows teaches us anything, it's that the color and texture of plants impact us all very deeply. Wind moving across prairie grasses, light dappling

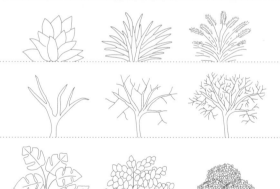

through the canopy of a sycamore tree, the peeling bark of a
birch tree, the delicate textures of ferns along a creek. We are,
in fact, hardwired to pay attention to these details. The word
biophilia describes the idea that humans have survived and
evolved by making connections with the natural world and
with living things in particular. Plants, wildlife, and the outdoors have been and remain essential to our well-being. Even
if we are increasingly urban and disconnected from natural
processes, we remain deeply sensitive to the colors and textures of the natural world around us.

We don't need an advanced degree in biology to intuitively
understand that what a plant looks like is related to where it's
from. We associate leafless succulents with the desert, and
large-leaved foliage with moist areas. We can also sense that
certain plant combinations feel more harmonious and adapted
to a place than others. Texture and color are powerful tools
because they play with these meanings and associations that
we *already* have with plants and landscapes:

> People may have multiple, complex, and often contradic-
> tory emotions with a single landscape. A dark woodland
> path may feel foreboding to some and beckoning to others.
> What we see in both responses is a moment of resonance, a
> pulling out of oneself to encounter a landscape directly. As
> designers, we cannot control what people will feel. But we
> can set the stage for these encounters.

Texture and color are influenced by many factors: a plant's
size, its health, neighboring plants, the distance they are
viewed from, the quality of light, and the time of year. Color
gets more attention than texture for the simple reason that it's
flashier, but texture is a more enduring characteristic of plants.
Colors, such as blooms, are often temporary.

The size, shape, and spacing of leaves are key in determining our perception of a plant's texture, although all parts of
the plant contribute throughout the seasons. Grouping similar
plant species together creates a larger homogenous texture:

OPPOSITE, LEFT
The coarse texture of date
palms contrasts with the
fine texture of grasses at
Flying Disc Ranch in Thermal,
California.

OPPOSITE, RIGHT
Contrasting plant textures
offer a dynamic, graceful
portrait at Maximilianpark in
Hamm, Germany.

OPPOSITE, BOTTOM
At the Huntington Botanical
Gardens, the fine texture of
deer grass (*Muhlenbergia
rigens*) harmonizes well
with the bolder texture of
rose mallee (*Eucalyptus
rhodantha*) and Mediterranean
spurge (*Euphorbia
characias*).

think of a single meadow grass versus a field of grasses, or the canopy of a forest when viewed from above. The texture of a plant or group of plants will also be impacted by the texture of the surrounding landscape and architecture. For example, a smooth wall can be used to bring out the texture of plants in front of it.

Plant textures are often described in terms of coarse, fine, and medium. Coarse textures are rougher and stand out individually. Their characteristics include thick branches, spines, large leaves, leaves with strong veins, variegated colors, and bold, loose forms. Think of monstera, agave, palm, hydrangea, acanthus, bird-of-paradise, rhododendrons, cannas, and hostas. Their bold structures create strong contrasts of light and dark, which our eyes are naturally drawn to.

The characteristics of fine-textured plants include small, delicate leaves and flowers; narrow trunks; tall, thin stems; and small twigs with many branches. These plants are often described as light, sprawling, or wispy. They include vines, grasses, ferns, Japanese maples, honey locust, asparagus, and love-in-a-mist. The leaves of some fine-textured plants, like boxwood, are densely packed and can be pruned into bold forms.

Medium-textured plants are, as you guessed it, in between, with medium-sized leaves and branches and an overall rounded form. They include agapanthus, camellia, pittosporum, viburnum, heuchera, and penstemon. The coarse, medium, and fine categories are relative—a medium-textured plant looks coarse next to a fine-textured one—and a coarse hardscape (e.g., with boulders) will minimize the texture of surrounding plants.

There is no right way to work with textures in a garden. One approach is to balance different textures in order to create a well-rounded, complex composition. Alternatively, we can have a dominant texture that works with secondary textures. For example, fine-textured plants, like grasses, can be grouped together to unify a garden space, creating a backdrop for different textures to pop.

Like texture, the color of a plant is relative to its surrounding, more saturated in summer sun and more subdued in winter light, brighter in the morning sun and deeper in late afternoon light. These colors impact us emotionally. Warm colors, like yellow, orange, and red, are energizing, while the cooler shades of blue, green, and violet are calming and soothing.

Color comes from all parts of a plant but varies throughout the seasons. Flowers get the most attention: some plants have a small number of large and colorful flowers, while others have

There is enough color and texture in the low-lying, salt-tolerant vegetation off the coast of Big Sur, California, to leave us in pure wonder.

The season and time of day influences the color and texture of plants, as in this frosty, winter sunrise in Germany.

an abundance of small flowers. Leaves also bring color: they can be variegated (with different colors on the same leaf), and, in the case of deciduous plants, change colors in the fall, often to dramatic effect. Fruit, branches, and bark can bring color too, as in the bark of redwood trees and the yellow specks in a lemon tree.

What parts of a plant have the most colorful changes throughout the year? Flowers bring color in the spring and summer, fruit and foliage in the fall, and the bark and branches of deciduous trees gain visibility in winter. One effective way

OPPOSITE
Color and perception impact
each other. Roughly three
thousand azalea plants of
different varieties bloom
outside Shiofune Kannon
Temple in Japan.

of coordinating all the changing colors in the garden—between flower, foliage, bark, and fruit—is to prepare a color calendar that sequences the changing plant colors throughout the year. Like texture, there is no one strategy to work with color. One is to use more subdued colors as a background for brighter, more saturated ones; another is to group plants of a specific color into drifts or masses.

Color and texture actually impact each other. The fewer textures in a planting, the more the variations in color will stand out. Conversely, the fewer the variety of colors, the more the textures will be apparent. Planting designers frequently plant in drifts or masses, grouping together plants with distinct colors and textures. But don't be afraid of breaking conventional wisdom. Attempt a wild rainbow of color and shapes. Experiment!

It's impossible to think about plants without the colors and textures that excite, inspire, and calm us. What's even more inspiring is that, as the clock turns and the seasons change, the appearance of plants evolves, offering us an ever-changing dance for our eyes. What a better invitation than to join the spectacle, engaging with the best sensory gifts the world has to offer us.

CHAPTER THIRTEEN

PLANTS—THE ECOSYSTEM PERSPECTIVE

If we were to design a garden based only on the size, color, and texture of plants, we would create a disaster. Think about it. We can make a list of plants that would look great together, and we can arrange them in very interesting ways, but if the plants are not adapted to the regional climate, to the microclimate of the garden, and to the other plants in the garden, then they simply will not thrive.

We make good planting decisions when three relationships are in harmony: the relationships of plants to people, plants to local climate, and plants to other plants in the garden. In the previous two chapters, we focused on strengthening the relationship between people and plants, by relating to plants spatially through size and shape and visually through color and texture. In this chapter, we are going to focus on relating plants to climate and to other plants. Our goal is to understand what makes plants thrive and how the garden can become a living ecosystem full of interdependent relationships between species. We want gardens rich in plant, animal, and fungal

OPPOSITE
Great gardens are thriving ecosystems, not just a collection of plants. A biodiverse garden grows from the decompacted asphalt of a former parking lot in this garden by Wagon Landscaping outside of Paris.

OPPOSITE, TOP
At the Ruth Bancroft Garden & Nursery in Walnut Creek, California, plants from all over the world coexist together because all are adapted to the hot Mediterranean climate.

OPPOSITE, BOTTOM
Plants in the wild are perfectly adapted to place. The shrubs in this Greek landscape evolved to be low and spiny in order to cope with strong winds and browsing animals.

life, adapted to local conditions and an increasingly volatile climate. We want gardens that feel alive and wild, that benefit other creatures and us at the same time. It's a win-win situation, but how do we get there?

Let's start by considering the garden as an ecosystem. An ecosystem is a biological community of interacting organisms and their physical environment. A healthy garden ecosystem means symbiotic relationships between living organisms (e.g., plants, people, wildlife, fungi, bacteria), nonliving materials (e.g., stone, plastic, metal), and the local environment. We want all the elements of a garden (e.g., people, plants, things, climate) to work together. For example, we want plants adapted to the site that will provide food and habitat for pollinating insects, thus we don't want toxic materials and products that would harm either the plants or the insects. A garden is resilient when it is home to many interdependent relationships between the parts of the garden. Think of a fabric. It's easy to tear when it's only composed of a few threads. But weave hundreds of threads together and the fabric becomes unbreakable.

Plants form the base of the food chain in nearly all ecosystems. So how are plants chosen to support an ecosystem? We have to understand their needs. Like people, plants thrive under certain optimal conditions, which include the intensity and duration of light, the availability of water, the type of soil, and the presence of other animals or plants on which the plant depends.

If in doubt about what a plant needs, we can look up the climate the plant has evolved in. Is it from moist meadows of the Great Plains, salty coasts of New England, or dry hillsides of the Sonoran Desert? These questions tell us what type of conditions the plant will be most adapted to. When we know what a plant likes, we can look at whether it is adapted to our region. The climate of a region is its long-term weather patterns. My climate in Northern California is Mediterranean with warm summers and no summer rainfall. But we need finer resolution than that. We also want to know about our local microclimate. Although my regional climate is Mediterranean, my

ABOVE
Plants adapted to growing in rocky cracks with very little soil grow in this alpine garden at Tilden Regional Park Botanic Garden.

OPPOSITE
On the Greek island of Antiparos, landscape architecture studio doxiadis+ uses vegetation native to the site to integrate the architecture into the landscape. Plants closer to the houses are planted at higher density. Farther away, the density of plantation decreases to allow for natural revegetation between the plants.

hometown of Oakland is a few degrees warmer than Berkeley to the north.

There can also be huge climatic variations within a garden. Buildings, fences, walls, hedges, trees, and ground material all impact the temperature and moisture of a site. For example, on a sunny day in the Northern Hemisphere the southern side of a house will be much warmer and drier than the northern side of a house, and on a windy day, the downwind side of a fence will be more still than the upwind side. Within the same garden, we can have microclimates that are worlds apart. We can use this to our advantage by using plants adapted to these varied conditions.

Gardens with many different microclimates—hot, cold, dry, wet, windy, still—can welcome a greater diversity of plant species and support relationships between these species. In contrast, a garden with the same condition everywhere (e.g., a flat lawn) will create a less diverse ecosystem. A fun way

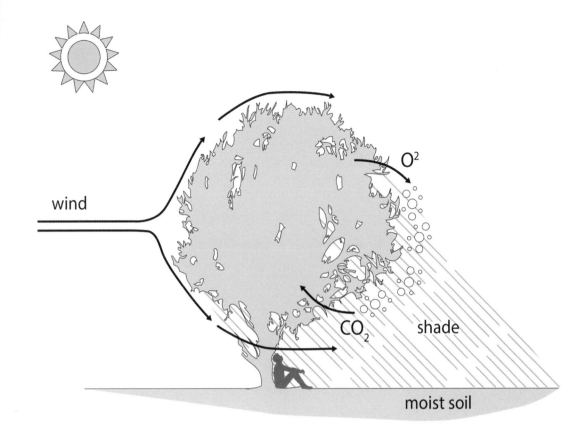

O^2

wind

CO_2

shade

moist soil

to welcome a high diversity of plants in the garden is to create many different microclimates using different materials.
Experimenting with soil, rocks, recycled concrete, gravel,
wood, and sand will create unique conditions for plants (and
wildlife) adapted to those conditions.

Plants don't just live in microclimates, they also create
them. A tree creates shade, which means cooler temperatures
and more moisture in the shaded soil. Specific plants will
thrive underneath that tree's shade. These plants, in turn,
create microclimates too. For example, in coastal Northern
California, redwood trees tower over rhododendron trees,
which grow above licorice fern, underneath which grow
mosses and lichens. We could keep on zooming in and in
endlessly. Each plant has a niche—a place and role within the

ABOVE
Plants don't just adapt to
microclimates, they create
them. A tree, for example,
redirects wind, creates shade,
keeps the soil moist, and
produces oxygen.

OPPOSITE
For thousands of years,
gardeners have tried growing
exotic plants from different
climates in the same place.
At the Hamilton Gardens
in New Zealand, the forest
is completely designed
by humans.

ecosystem—and is adapted to the unique conditions of that niche. Being aware of microclimates and niches allows us to understand whether our plant choices are adapted to a site and capable of forming a functioning community.

Luckily, we all have great teachers: the natural landscapes around us and the plants that grow spontaneously in them. Wherever we go, we can see how plants build relations. Whether we are in protected areas like forests and meadows, or along the sides of a railroad track, we can observe how and where plants are growing. Which plants are the most common? The tallest and shortest? Are specific species attracted to specific micro-conditions? Observing in this way, we notice how perfectly every plant finds its place, its niche, within its surroundings.

Our planting decisions can mimic the naturally existing plant communities we see in the world. Inspiration from nature can allow us to not only choose plant combinations that look well together but also to ensure that these plants benefit each other. One way to do this is to think of plant communities as occurring in three layers.

First, the structural layer is composed of large plants that create the main visual structure of the scene. These can be trees, shrubs, and large perennials. They are long-lived and have distinctive shapes. Second, the seasonal theme layer is composed of plants that are mid-height and become visually dominant seasonally because of their color or texture. Third, the ground-cover layer is composed of low, shade-tolerant species, whose primary purpose is to cover the ground between taller species, much as one would use mulch. This last layer is key; plants in this layer often do not have striking forms or colorful flowers—and are often hidden underneath the other layers—but they provide erosion control, weed suppression, and pollen for insects. They go beyond creating a visually appealing plant community, to creating a functional, symbiotic plant community.

These three layers can be used to mimic various types of ecosystems. To mimic an open grassland community, there is

OPPOSITE, TOP
At the Jardin de Vasterival in Normandy, France, trees, mid-sized, and ground-cover plants exist harmoniously in the same space because each is adapted to its niche in the ecosystem.

OPPOSITE, BOTTOM
A lawn winds its way through plants adapted to moist air and low-light conditions of the coastal forest at the Jardin de Vasterival in Normandy, France.

emphasis on the middle layer with a few scattered plants in the structural layer. For a mixed woodland-shrubland community, we might clump structural plants and mid-layer plants to create patches of shrubs and trees. And for an open forest community, the structural and ground-cover layers are highlighted.

Words like *layers*, *communities*, *microclimate*, and *symbiosis* are all ways of describing how plants relate to their broader ecosystem. Understanding gardens as ecosystems gives us the tool to create diverse, dynamic, resilient worlds, with spellbinding results. Symbiosis is a win-win: the more we admire and nurture the plant communities around us, the more we realize that we too are part of those communities.

CHAPTER FOURTEEN

COMMUNITY— GROWING RELATIONSHIPS WITH WILDLIFE

OPPOSITE, TOP
A common hedgehog emerges from a tunnel, part of a hedgehog superhighway that connects over sixty properties in the village of Kirtlington, England. This photo was taken at night— when hedgehogs are active— with motion-activated flash photography.

OPPOSITE, BOTTOM
The world's first known hedgehog staircase was built to accommodate the difference in ground elevations between two adjacent gardens. Hedgehogs used it the very first night it was installed.

The small village of Kirtlington in England is home to the country's most famous hedgehog highway. A network of CD-sized holes, cut into walls and fences, links sixty properties in the village and allows the native hedgehog population to move from one garden to the next. Gardens are great habitats for hedgehogs, but fences and walls make it difficult for them to move around, look for food, and find mates, and the British hedgehog population has declined by 90 percent since World War II. Kirtlington's hedgehog superhighway features some truly creative hedgehog architecture, including miniature ramps, staircases, and decorative portals.

Kirtlington reminds us that, regardless of their location, gardens are always connected to the wider landscape and its inhabitants. Even a small balcony in a high-rise is connected to the wider region by the air, which carries plant pollen, fungal spores, and birds. For better or worse, raccoons, blue jays, and butterflies are not concerned with property lines. For them, our gardens are more habitat, a place to forage, nest, and play.

Hedgehog architecture in Kirtlington: a ramp bridges the three-foot elevation change between two gardens.

Our surprise at seeing other creatures inhabiting our gardens demonstrates the limits of our perspective. Anthropocentrism is the view of the world in which humans are at the center. The alternative to anthropocentrism is ecocentrism, in which humans are just one among many species, each with its own dignity and place.

Sharing space with other species matters—not because of what other species do for us, but because they simply exist. Sharing is not always easy. There can be conflict: deer and gophers eat our plants, and house cats hunt native birds. We do not have to love all the wildlife in our gardens, but we do have to recognize their right to exist, their unique way of being in the world. The goal of this chapter is to challenge the assumption that the garden is only for us. We want to navigate our relations with other species with intelligence and empathy. Perhaps the first step to welcoming wildlife in our gardens is simply to understand their needs, which unsurprisingly are the same as ours: shelter, food, and water. By researching the

Many small bird species enjoy the protection of thickets and hedges. Here, an American tree sparrow (*Spizelloides arborea*) rests in a willow and dogwood thicket near Bozeman, Montana.

specific needs of wildlife and providing for those needs, our garden becomes a genuinely shared space.

Wildlife need to feel safe in their surroundings, so they often seek physical spaces that screen them visually and physically from potential predators. For example, many birds enjoy the protection of plant branches and foliage. However, different bird species have different needs, so they gravitate toward specific plants or parts of plants. Song sparrows love the inside of thickets and shrubs, but they also like to forage in leaf litter on the ground, where they can find crawling insects for food. Warblers, however, prefer being higher up in the canopy of trees, where they can hunt flying insects. In contrast, the mourning dove, like many butterflies and lizards, prefers open areas with some bare ground and small plants, and avoids dense vegetation. By planting in layers—ground cover, shrub, and tree—and by allowing leaf litter to remain on the ground, we provide habitats that meet the needs of all three bird species. Planting in layers also shapes lines of sight in the garden; it's a strategy that both provides for the needs of other species and satisfies practical human concerns.

Plants play a particularly important role in the garden ecosystem by attracting insects, which in turn feed the rest of the food chain. By incorporating plants that grow and bloom at different times throughout the year, we can provide insects and their predators with a consistent source of food throughout the year.

Many insects have evolved to depend exclusively on certain plants. Monarch caterpillars, for example, feed only on milkweed plants. Growing the native plants on which local insect populations have evolved thus helps provide essential habitat for those insects. Having said that, non-native plants also provide crucial habitat. Studies have even found that some non-native plantings can attract an equal or greater abundance of insects than native species. As a general rule, it's best to prioritize native plants but non-natives can also be used as long as they aren't invasive, taking over a given area and preventing other plants from growing.

A wooden house offers shelter to ducks in Oranjewoud, Netherlands.

Insects have evolved to use the shelters found in nature—living plants, leaf litter, seed heads, dead stems, rotting logs, and rocks. When we tidy up our gardens too much, we remove these nooks and crannies. Seventy percent of the world's bee species actually nest underground, and they need access to the soil. Instead of covering a garden in mulch, consider using ground-cover plants and letting leaf litter accumulate. Many insects, like moths and butterflies, overwinter in the fallen leaves of plants that many homeowners love removing. To avoid a messy look, it's possible to clean up only a few of the more visible areas of the garden, and simply let the rest be until early spring.

A fantastic way to attract solitary insects (those that live alone) is to build an insect hotel. These structures can be packed with recycled materials that provide shelter for insects. Native bees for example love hollow stems and holes drilled

Minimally managing parts of our gardens and sowing native wildflower seeds are two strategies to provide habitat for insects and wildlife. Here, a meadow of Oregon sunshine (*Eriophyllum lanatum*) and California poppy (*Eschscholzia californica*) in an Oregon vineyard.

in wood, with different sized holes attracting different bee species. Bird houses, feeders, and bird baths, and doors at the bottom of fences and walls are other simple interventions that invariably attract wildlife.

Ponds play a crucial role in attracting wildlife by providing habitat for insects. Designing ponds with variable depths and alternating the pond edge with sand, rocks, gravel, and soil creates microhabitats welcoming to a diversity of insects, amphibians, and plants. Planting in and around a pond, and piling rocks around the edge, can help screen amphibians from predators such as cats and larger birds. And incorporating a gentle slope on part of the pond's edge allows animals to get out of the water in case they fall in.

A lot of these strategies involve shifting our assumptions about what is useful and beautiful for us, to what is useful and beautiful for us *and* others. Accepting messiness and conflict

is part of the process—as it is with any relationship. We have to find solutions that respect all species' right to live, and we must cultivate awareness of the cultural baggage that we bring into the situation. For example, our fear of common urban species, such as rats, mice, raccoons, and possums, has more to do with our own insecurities than the actual dangers and inconveniences they pose. Instead of acting out of fear, we can act out of curiosity and empathy.

It's crucial to give ourselves the time and space to actually observe the wildlife in our gardens, to sit down on a bench or on the ground quietly for five minutes and see who arrives.

A five-star insect hotel adds character to the Rose Garden at the Parc de Cervantes in Barcelona. It's important to replace the nesting materials periodically to prevent insect diseases or one species from taking over.

A greater variety of micro-ecosystems in a garden will attract a greater diversity of wildlife.

We can identify which insects are pollinating which flowers, and start to differentiate between the different types of bees in the garden. You can keep records of bird, mammal, and insect sightings, and write down the dates of observation. Trail cams are a fascinating way to see what happens in the garden when we are away or sleeping. I cannot tell you how much I enjoy the videos of mice and possums enjoying my garden at night.

I have been careful to not provide a list of reasons why we should care for other forms of life. We care for other human beings because they are here with us in this world. The same goes for other species. Caring means digging into the practical details of what others actually need. Understanding the needs of wildlife and providing for them is the first step. Humans have so much to learn. May we bring more life, more flaps, flips, croaks, and buzzes to our gardens.

CHAPTER FIFTEEN

COMMUNITY— GROWING RELATIONSHIPS WITH PEOPLE

The Princess Gardens grows in the heart of downtown Berlin. Stepping off the noisy street, one enters what appears to be a parallel dimension: people gardening in planter beds, attending workshops for activists, or sitting in the sun drinking coffee. And then there are the crops: orange, red, and black fruits grow tall on tomato plants that stretch on handmade wooden trellises; different potato varieties grow in rice sacks; an endless array of vegetables, including turnips, radishes, fennel, kale, carrots, and purslane, as well as edible spontaneous plants, such as dandelion, nasturtium, and borage, all grow out of buckets, crates, and bags. Signs announce which vegetables are ready for harvest and when visitors can work in the garden. A group of twenty or so have gathered for a workshop on seed harvesting. In the dappled shade of a grove of locust trees, cooks are busy preparing meals from plants harvested in the garden, and a garden bar offers drinks. Plastic crates are stacked as tables and chairs for visitors to sit and enjoy the space. All the food plants grow in movable containers and

beds so that the entire garden is mobile. Even the garden bar, kitchen, and the stall that sells seedlings in recycled Tetra Paks are housed in shipping containers.

But it's the social aspect that makes the Princess Gardens unique: it's a place that promotes interaction between people. Walking through the garden, one sees all types of social interactions: a family sharing tips and strategies on plant care as they water the vegetables, a couple basking in the sun, and strangers introducing themselves at the beginning of a workshop. The garden's users are representative of Berlin's diverse community: local residents, tourists, and others who seem to just stumble upon the place.

The vibe at the Princess Gardens is decidedly activist. Formally organized as a social enterprise, the garden is run by paid staff and a core group of volunteers. Its primary aim is to make the garden a public center of learning and sharing for all the city's residents. The explicitly democratic approach is intended to make the garden a laboratory for radical experimentation, a place where sustainability, biodiversity, job creation, zero waste, healthy eating, and environmental justice

LEFT
The over three hundred gardens at the Tempelhof Field in Berlin are managed by local residents but open to the public.

RIGHT
The creative use of materials at the Tempelhof gardens leads to garden features with sculptural qualities, such as this leaning planter.

A GARDEN'S PURPOSE

can not only be discussed but also implemented. As stated on the garden's website, "In an unobtrusive and pragmatic way, such gardens raise the question of how we want to live in our cities in the future."

A few miles away, on a little over an acre of land at the eastern end of Berlin's former Tempelhof Airport, lies an inviting, low-lying sprawl of garden plots. The roughly three hundred plots are allocated to local residents, but remain open to the public. Recycled and reclaimed objects are everywhere—all nailed, painted, and strung together by hand. Bathtubs double as planter beds, plastic scraps are reimagined as windmills. Wood pallets create inviting spaces to sit and rest on. Local residents tend the plots, turning them into cute refuges full of personality, but they don't own them. The absence of fences creates a welcoming feel to the place. Here too, friends and families gather for picnics, strangers congregate around a group of musicians, and tourists take naps. This openness is relaxing, lowering people's defenses, offering opportunities for connection.

As these two examples from Berlin demonstrate, gardens are not just green spaces that look beautiful in photographs. They are places that nurture the essential human need for social connection. Gardens, in addition to being a home for plants and wildlife, are a home for people. They are places where community members interact, where cultural identity can be forged, and where intimate, comprehensible relationships are created within the concrete jungle. They also provide breathing room for those without access to green spaces. Gardens appeal to people across demographic lines, so they can promote interactions between those who don't usually meet or socialize, including people from different racial, religious, and ethnic backgrounds. They are intergenerational, with older gardeners passing on farming techniques or recipes to younger members.

And of course, gardens are where we grow food. Many immigrants and refugees have trouble finding their favorite foods in local stores, or they simply cannot afford them. What

OPPOSITE, TOP
Syrian refugees harvest seeds of coreopsis at Buzuruna Juzuruna, an educational farm in Lebanon dedicated to safeguarding the farming and horticultural traditions of Syrian refugees.

OPPOSITE, LEFT
Gardens invite us to connect with the natural world. In places like the Ersal Syrian refugee camp in Lebanon, they provide a sense of home.

OPPOSITE, RIGHT
A garden, designed by and for the homeless community that lives underneath Interstate 880 in Oakland, California. Gardens provide marginalized individuals and oppressed populations a vital means to interact with natural processes.

we eat is inherently linked to how we define ourselves. Gardens provide space for individuals and families living far from their native lands to grow the foods and medicines that are both meaningful to them and necessary for them in maintaining a sense of identity in a foreign environment. Growing and cooking these foods is a way of nurturing one's traditions and spirituality in the face of challenging, often tragic, circumstances.

For many, gardens are some of the *only* places where they have the freedom to express themselves. Oakland, California—which has one of the highest rates of homelessness in the US—is home to an abundance of gardens cultivated by homeless individuals and groups. They are located in public parks, along the side of the road, and by train tracks. Made with found and recycled objects, from milk crates, shopping carts, carpets, buckets, and bicycle wheels, they are cultivated with tremendous care and passion. They create a sense of home. These gardens are in many ways some of the most powerful. Made by individuals experiencing grave societal injustices, their existence despite these injustices speaks to the power of gardens and gardening as basic tools of survival, a way of affirming one's existence in a system that actively ignores that existence.

We learn from gardens because they help us ask important questions toward dreaming up the world of tomorrow. School gardens play an important role in helping students develop a connection to nature from an early age. When we understand the value of nature, we work tirelessly to protect it. School gardens are essential tools in this way to empower the next generation.

Starting in 2008, at the Chisungu Primary School in Zimbabwe, sixth and seventh graders were interested in how to dispose of human waste in an environmentally friendly way. With limited resources, they decided to build a pit toilet and planted trees around it. Eventually the trees' roots will be fed by the contents of the pit, transforming human waste into shade and vegetation. The students also ran scientific trials to see how urine from the boy's urinal could be used as a fertilizer. They discovered that urine leads to significant

Gardens are places to learn together. At the Chisungu Primary School in Zimbabwe, students conducted trials to test the impact of urine on the growth of spinach.

At the Chisungu School, a ring of gum trees planted around a pit toilet will eventually tap into the pit's waste and provide shade to the toilet.

Harvesting green vegetables in a front yard in Salinas, California. Working in the garden is an opportunity to build new relationships, strengthen old ones, and have fun.

increases in the production of corn, green vegetables, and trees. Chisungu's gardens don't just provide practical solutions to everyday challenges; they empower schoolchildren by giving them a shared and common goal. For the rest of their lives, these students will be able to visit the trees that they nurtured.

Just as gardens can be home for wildlife, they can be home for humans too. These community gardens—for immigrants, those without homes, and students—are places where our deepest collective wounds are cared for and nurtured. They point to a future that does not exclude human beings, where loving community is not a privilege, but a basic human right. The garden is where healing can begin.

CHAPTER SIXTEEN

SOIL—WORKING FROM THE GROUND UP

OPPOSITE
This wild garden by Wagon Landscaping in the Aubervilliers suburb of Paris grows in only a few inches of soil placed in between decompacted asphalt and above an impermeable base of concrete.

In 2016 in the city of Aubervilliers, outside Paris, the designers of Wagon Landscaping decided to transform a former parking lot measuring seventeen thousand square feet—slated for eventual development—into a nature observatory. The asphalt had already been torn up, but underneath it was an impermeable layer of concrete that they could not remove. Anything they did on the site would have to exist on top of this concrete layer. They wondered: What would happen if they did nothing but add soil, seedlings, and seeds to the site? Would plants thrive in just a few inches of soil here and there? Could this place become a biodiverse ecosystem?

Inspired by the nineteenth-century European tradition of building alpine gardens in rocky soil, the Wagon team spread thirteen hundred cubic feet of soil and five hundred cubic feet of gravel onto the site. In this incredibly shallow soil and over the course of five days, they planted one thousand perennials, two thousand sedum, one hundred trees, and sowed two pounds of seeds. In line with their philosophy of creative

OPPOSITE, TOP LEFT
Sites with poor or little soil are ideal for plants that evolved with these conditions, such as this common mullein (*Verbascum thapsus*) growing in almost pure asphalt and gravel.

OPPOSITE, TOP RIGHT
The Aubervilliers garden pictured before the addition of soil.

OPPOSITE, BOTTOM
Wagon Landscaping's planting and sowing decisions focused on plants adapted to presence of very little soil, including the non-native tree of heaven (*Ailanthus altissima*), a few of which are visible in the mid-ground.

resourcefulness, no materials were taken off the site and nothing received any irrigation. At first the plants grew slowly, little pockets of green amid patches of asphalt and dirt. Over the years, it has grown into a colorful, spontaneous garden, a place to observe how much plants can do with a bare minimum of soil.

Soil is the foundation of life in the garden! It's not just the ground on which we stand, our constant frame of reference. It feeds plants that serve as the foundation of the food chain in almost all ecosystems. Because we live above ground, it's hard to wrap our heads around the fact that soil is a living, dynamic ecosystem. A teaspoon of rich garden soil can hold up to one billion bacteria, several yards of fungal filaments, and thousands of protozoa. A square foot of healthy agricultural soil is typically home to up to one hundred arthropods, dozens of earthworms, not to mention mice, voles, shrews, other large animals, and the roots of plants. The vast majority of plants depend on soil-dwelling fungi to stay alive, with the fungi supplying minerals to the plants and the plants providing sugars to the fungi. In short, the soil underneath our feet is actually a food web whose members feed, and feed on, each other. From a biological and visual point of view, soil constitutes the foundation of our gardens.

What does this mean practically for our gardens? We can modify an existing soil to make it more hospitable for what we want to grow, for example by amending it with sand, gravel, and organic matter, inoculating it with fungal spores, or physically decompacting it with a shovel or rototiller. We can also choose plants adapted to the soil as it is. Hard clay soils, for example, can be notoriously challenging to work with, but vegetables like daikon radish, artichoke, and sunflowers thrive in them and will help decompact the clay. We can also create our own nutrient-dense soils at home by composting home and garden waste. The point is, as mentioned, to veer away from prescribing a specific way of working with soil, but instead to awaken curiosity and encourage experimentation.

With important exceptions like epiphytes, which don't need soil at all, all plants need soil from which they gain the organic matter and minerals they need. Plants thrive in specific soils they are adapted to, so we must begin by understanding different soil types. Important soil characteristics include texture (fine or coarse), structure (the different layers in the soil), how it holds and drains water, and the presence of nutrients and organic matter. Different ecosystems (e.g., forest, agricultural fields, prairies) have radically different soils. The soils in river valleys, for example, tend to be rich in organic matter and mineral contents as rivers and streams deposit soil on the valley floor. In contrast, soils on hilltop are usually more gravelly and lower in organic matter, as rain over time carries finer soil particles downhill.

When we think of soil in a garden, we generally imagine a dark, rich, fluffy soil. But there is in fact no one ideal soil since different plants like different soils. Some plants—like the majority of vegetables and fruits—do, indeed, like rich,

LEFT
Decompacted asphalt and gravel, mixed with imported soil, create a hybrid soil for this design by Wagon Landscaping in a Parisian courtyard.

RIGHT
The twelve-thousand-square-foot green roof of Howlett Hall at the Ohio State University is home to a dozen varieties of sedum, yarrow, fescue, thyme, alliums, and more. The soil on most of the roof is four to six inches thick, with some areas mounding to eighteen inches.

moist soils. Others—such as plants adapted to Mediterranean climates and rocky, gravelly conditions—will suffer in these same conditions because they prefer low organic matter. A frequent mistake of gardeners around the world is to take species that are adapted to poor soils (e.g., lavender, rosemary, thyme), plant them in rich soil, and overwater them. Although the plants typically grow fast, their roots don't mature well and they will be more prone to disease.

In such projects as the one that opened this chapter, there may be no soil at all on a site, so it has to be brought in. These projects are interesting because they are essentially creating a soil ecosystem from scratch. Green roofs, for example, require gardens to be created in just inches of soil. Because most roofs are not designed to handle the weight of significant soil and water, most green roofs only have a very thin layer of soil. The plants chosen for these soils *must* have shallow roots and be adapted to extreme conditions, and a whole industry has developed to make this possible: mats of sedum and mosses on less than two inches of soil are commercially available for green roofs.

Other ways of creating soil ecosystems take more time. In the fall of 2020, a dear friend and I decided to transform her family's suburban front lawn in Salinas, California, into a vegetable garden. The only problem was that the soil of the roughly one-thousand-square-foot lawn was hard compacted clay and covered by a thick, fibrous layer of Bermuda grass. To grow vegetables, we needed a rich, fluffy soil with no grass. We decided to "sheet mulch" the lawn. We spread four inches of compost over the lawn, covered it with recycled cardboard boxes (the "sheets"), and then covered the cardboard with four inches of mulch.

Over the course of the next few months, the existing soil and compost began to mix, as earthworms and other soil microorganisms moved from the soil into the compost. The cardboard suffocated and killed the Bermuda grass, which then decomposed and fed the soil. With rain, the cardboard broke down, leaving the mulch to cover the underlying soil and serve

TOP
A dried-out lawn in Salinas, California, with hard, compacted clay soil.

MIDDLE
Roughly four inches of imported compost are laid on top of the lawn.

BOTTOM
Recycled boxes are unfolded, tape and plastic labels are removed, and the flattened boxes are placed on top of the compost layer. Another four inches of mulch are later added.

ABOVE
Pictured is the Salinas garden,
exactly seven months after
the initial sheet mulching, with
vegetable garden and native
Californian hedge.

as a source of organic matter for the soil. The following spring, we planted dozens of species of kale, broccoli, cauliflower, and lettuce on the former lawn, as well as a hedge of California natives to serve as a buffer between the lawn and the sidewalk.

Why didn't we just spread a thick layer of compost and plant into that? Because we wanted the existing soil and the small amount of added compost to be integrated into a connected ecosystem of insects, bacteria, fungi, solids, liquids, and gases. That integration takes time. Although this approach requires preparation, once the compost, cardboard, and mulch have been added, the soil and its inhabitants do all the work.

Take a look at the plants growing spontaneously in pavement cracks near your home. These are gardens growing with barely any soil at all. We tend to underestimate the power of soil because it is the most invisible to us. Recognizing it as a living, diverse ecosystem helps us understand why it is so powerful. That power provides opportunities everywhere we look.

CHAPTER SEVENTEEN
WATER—ORCHESTRATING MOISTURE

OPPOSITE, TOP
At Springside Chestnut Hill Academy outside of Philadelphia, artist Stacy Levy used blue and transparent PVC piping to make rainfall exciting and important.

OPPOSITE, BOTTOM
After leaving the downspouts, rainfall flows through runnels carved in flagstone and into the rain garden.

At Springside Chestnut Hill Academy, a few miles west of Philadelphia, Pennsylvania, artist Stacy Levy has managed to make the drainage of water something to wonder about. Typically, when rain falls on a roof, it is directed into a gutter, down vertical downspouts, into municipal stormwater systems and local streams. Instead of the usual dull downspouts, Levy used blue PVC pipes and rearranged them into playful geometries. Where the pipes cross windows, she used transparent tubing that allows students to see the water flowing.

Exiting the pipes, rainwater splashes onto stone and concrete runnels before flowing through a bioswale (a trench planted with plants, designed to accommodate water runoff) toward a rain garden, where it soaks into the ground. Without the rain garden, rainfall on the roof would drain into the local Wissahickon Creek, which drains to the Schuylkill River and then to the Atlantic. Levy's design allows rain to percolate into the ground, so it can recharge the local water table and provide moisture to plants long after the rains have stopped.

The design also makes the movement of water fun, interesting, and something to reflect on. The curved blue pipes catch the eyes of pedestrians and people driving by. We usually pipe and channel water invisibly toward us, for our sinks, showers, and hoses, and then invisibly away from us. Our buildings and cities are generally designed to drain water away: modern civilization has a history of draining swamps, channeling rivers, and paving over soils. Levy calls this "people everywhere; rain in narrow spaces." We've paved over so much ground that runoff gets concentrated into channels, which leads to flooding. Groundwater, in turn, is depleted, making drought and fires more likely, and the lack of moisture in the ground causes us to over-irrigate our gardens.

Rain gardens are located lower relative to their surroundings, in order to allow water to drain naturally, as seen here at the Arlington National Cemetery.

Curb cuts allow stormwater to drain into rain gardens and bioswales, preventing the flooding of homes and streets.

Water matters. Life revolves around it. To stand in a garden is to stand surrounded by moving water: the root tips of a plant absorb moisture, draw it upward to its leaves, and eventually release it through their leaves as vapor. Given its importance, how can we reevaluate our relationship with water in the garden? Garden wisdom is filled with generalities about watering—"don't water at midday," "don't wet leaves," or "water this many times per week." These rules may be accurate, but following them blindly prevents us from becoming keen observers of our surroundings and learning for ourselves.

There are, for instance, many ways of watering plants. Sprinklers of all kinds—including oscillating sprinklers, impact sprinklers, and micro sprinklers—spread water relatively evenly over a given surface area. In contrast, drip irrigation—which includes drip tape, drip emitters, and soaker hoses—focuses water delivery on specific areas, usually at the foot of a plant, and is a popular way to conserve water. Irrigation timers allow us to automate the watering process without us having to be there.

These tools, however, only work if we are attuned to the needs of our plants. Automating the process takes us away from the satisfying, intuitive experience of learning directly from the plants. Watering by hand invites us to observe our plants. Going from plant to plant definitely takes time, but the process can hopefully encourage us to grow plants adapted to a garden's natural rainfall.

What are we looking for when deciding how to water our plants? The soil is a good place to start. Soil texture plays a crucial role in determining plants' watering needs. In porous soils (e.g., those with a lot of sand and gravel), water drains quickly and leaches nutrients away from the roots. Finer, heavier soils (e.g., those with a lot of clay) saturate more quickly; watering them too quickly will cause water to run off the surface and away from the plant. As we've discussed, plants are adapted to different types of soils. Grouping plants into areas according to their water needs makes it easier to design their soil and irrigate them appropriately (these areas are called hydrozones).

Mediterranean herbs, for example, thrive in drier soils compared to leafy greens like lettuce. Plant thyme and lettuce together, and either the thyme will get too much water or the lettuce not enough.

We can look for signs of under watering and overwatering in plants. The leaves of a plant that requires a well-drained soil will start browning at the tips and eventually die if there is too much moisture. But when observing plants for signs of illness, it's important to not jump to conclusions too quickly: leaves losing their firmness (i.e., wilting) can be a sign that a plant needs water. But it could also signal root disease, stem borers, extreme heat, or too much water. It all depends on context.

Topography plays a major role in directing water. Because water flows downhill, a berm or a mound holds water back, whereas a swale or depression lets water in. Rain gardens are located in sunken areas so they accumulate moisture. The top

A stone-filled trench in this backyard absorbs water from its surroundings and channels it downslope.

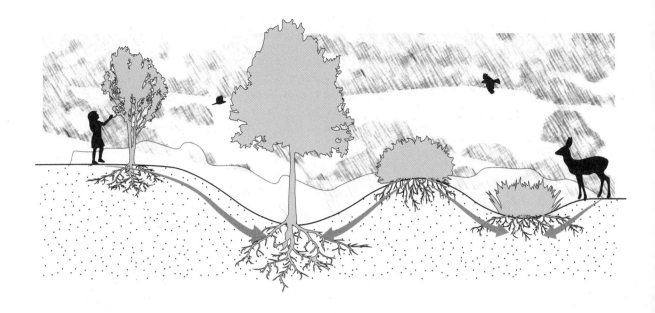

Because water flows downhill, topography is a simple and powerful way to redirect rainfall. Moisture-loving plants thrive at the bottom of swales whilst those that prefer more drainage thrive at the top of berms.

of an earthen berm is drier than the bottom of the mound, so moisture-loving plants enjoy the bottom of the mound, whereas plants that enjoy well-draining soils prefer the top.

To conserve water and make watering easier in the garden, we can place small berms around a plant that channels water toward the base of the plant, helping the water soak into the ground toward the plant's roots. Essentially the inverse of a raised bed, this technique is used in dry climates around the world to prevent water evaporation, protect plants against wind and sand, and increase shading.

Whether we live in the desert or the rainforest, there are endless benefits to designing systems that allow rainwater to percolate into the soil instead of municipal stormwater systems. Terraces, rain gardens, bioswales, and retention ponds all slow down the movement of water, giving it time to seep into the ground. They limit the need for irrigation in a garden, create habitat for wildlife, and reduce flooding potential. They also allow pollutants, such as oils and metals that cars release, to break down in the soil rather than contaminate river systems. Most importantly, by making the movement of water visible and beautiful, rainwater systems help us value it.

ABOVE
Water conservation tools and equipment can be beautiful, like these barrels that collect rainfall in Lancaster, Pennsylvania.

RIGHT
Planting on top of a mound, which has better drainage than the bottom, gives gardeners and farmers more control over the moisture levels for their plants, as seen with these eggplant seedlings.

OPPOSITE
The Zuni people of what is today called Arizona and New Mexico have traditionally used "waffle gardens" to conserve moisture in the arid climate. Here, a contemporary Zuni waffle garden by Curtis Quam.

For those who can afford it, it's easy to turn on the faucet without wondering where the water comes from. We can get complacent and forget how dependent on water we are. In Los Angeles, the roof of a nine-hundred-square-foot house can, in an average rain year, collect 7,200 gallons of water—that's thirty-eight year's worth of drinking water, or enough water to irrigate five hundred fruit trees annually. Numbers such as these—in a city that only gets about twelve inches of rain annually—should make us pause and ask: How can we build more meaningful relationships with the element that sustains us all?

We can collect rainwater for home use. We can use gray-water (water coming from the kitchen, washers, and shower) for irrigation. And we can incorporate rain gardens into our homes. We can also explore ways to celebrate water, like Stacy Levy's blue downspouts. The opportunities are endless.

EPILOGUE

To enter a garden is to experience the fundamentally magical nature of reality. Walking up to the trunk of a large tree, we can put our hands on its bark and feel the multicolored lichens that carpet its surface. We can close our eyes and listen to its leaves rustling in the wind. We can watch birds and other wildlife flying and climbing in and out of its canopy. Surrounded by life forms so different from us, and yet whose beauty we appreciate effortlessly, we are drawn out of our own bubbles, reawakening to the colorful, exuberant, and multitextured world in which we live.

Walking through an abandoned industrial lot, on soil heavy with toxins, we can notice weeds growing in between the cracks in the asphalt, vines growing up a chain link fence, and moss thriving in the shallow layers of urban dust. Regardless of where we look, we always find the presence of other living beings growing and dying, and the energizing powers of the natural elements, including light, wind, and rain. The possibility for wonder is everywhere.

In cities, the countryside, and everywhere in between, gardens bring families, friends, and neighbors together. To observe people from all walks of life sharing the same deep connection to nature is a much-needed reminder that our commonalities are so much more powerful, and interesting, than our differences.

In the end, gardens are magical because they are places where we focus our attention on the diversity, beauty, and fragility of our landscapes, cultures, and planet. They are powerful because they are real. They open us to the exuberant, sensory world in which we live, the world of birch bark and pine resin, of cawing ravens and burbling creeks, of sandstone, thunderstorms, birth, and decay. It's the exposure to all of that that makes gardens such grounding places to be.

Gardens promote presence. We feel present in ourselves and we feel the presence of others—other people, other beings, other elements. Unlike screens, which mediate perception, gardens offer us direct interaction with the natural world. And unlike social media, which promotes a frictionless socialization, gardening is full of friction, placing us amid the weeds, dirtying our clothing, and forcing us to honestly, though not always gracefully, engage the world head-on.

And that is the invitation of gardens, and of this book: to joyfully and imaginatively turn our attention to the miraculous, mysterious, dusty, rambunctious world we live in; and to wake up to the understanding that we are all an essential part of this magic, not apart from it.

ACKNOWLEDGMENTS

A book is like a young seedling that sprouts from seed after years immersed in the darkness and moisture of soil, leaves, insects, and mycorrhizae. It's the ecosystem that writes the book, not the individual.

I thank the land that has welcomed me throughout the research and writing of this book. This land, currently known as Oakland, California, is the traditional, unceded territory of the Ohlone people. Thank you, beautiful landscape and the Ohlone stewards, for providing such a nurturing home for the study of gardens, plant life, and life in general. The San Francisco Bay Area is full of fantastic small gardens that have served as my main laboratory of observation.

I thank UC Berkeley's Department of Landscape Architecture, where I completed my master's degree and which provided me with a little bit of structure to frame my chaotic thinking around nature and culture. In particular, thanks to Daphne Edwards, who taught my course on plant identification and got me hooked on plants, Chip Sullivan, for remaining young at heart, and Randy Hester, whose book *The Meaning of Gardens* was my first exposure to the idea that gardens are much more than gardens, that they are places and metaphors where we attempt to create a better world. Thank you, also, to Jennifer Wolch for our wonderful conversation on more-than-human design, as well to the staff at Blake Gardens for their welcome.

Thank you Julia Watson for our brief time working together and for inspiring me with her book *Lo-TEK*. After reading *Lo-TEK*, I became interested in how nature-based solutions translated into the daily life of residential homeowners.

Thank you David Godshall, principal at Terremoto, and Georgina Reid, founder of *Wonderground* journal, for encouraging my early attempts at writing about landscape in a way that was smart but accessible and warm. You guys rock.

Big thanks to Jennifer Jewell, who runs the podcast/website Cultivating Place, who took the time to offer her advice on the process of writing a book. And thanks to Caitlin Atkinson, photographer extraordinaire, who shared many of the photos included in this book.

I extend my gratitude to Julian Raxworthy, whose book *Overgrown* was another inspiration in my intellectual development. Julian's book taught me that design and the living world can and should empower each other. Thank you Julian for focusing our attention on the living qualities of our world.

Thank you to my friends Megan, Rose, Eric, and Allen, who support me rain or shine. And thank you, finally, to MaFe Gonzalez, to whom this book is dedicated.

CREDITS

Front cover: Félix de Rosen
Back cover: Félix de Rosen
4: Félix de Rosen
6: Yann Monel
7: Caitlin Atkinson
10: depositphotos.com
13 (left): Terremoto
13 (right): Yann Monel
15 (top): Félix de Rosen
15 (bottom): Daniel Jolivet, Flickr
16: Christopher Baker
18: Terremoto
19: depositphotos.com
20: Eric Sander
22: DXR, Wikimedia
25 (top): Terremoto
25 (bottom): Félix de Rosen
26: Allan Harris, Flickr
27: Yann Monel
28 (top): depositphotos.com
28 (left): onnola, Flickr
28 (right): Félix de Rosen
31 (top): depositphotos.com
31 (bottom): Big Cypress National Preserve, Flickr
32: Eric Sander
34–41: Félix de Rosen
42: Marion Brenner
44 (top): Terremoto
44 (bottom): Félix de Rosen
46: Caitlin Atkinson
48 (left): Caitlin Atkinson
48 (right and bottom): Félix de Rosen
51: Félix de Rosen
52 (top): Caitlin Atkinson
52 (bottom): Tibo Dhermy
54 (top): Dennis Sylvester Hurd, Flickr
54 (bottom): Matt Donham and Phoebe Lickwar
56–57: Eric Sander
58: Raafi Rivero
59 (top): Eric Sander
59 (bottom): Caitlin Atkinson
60: Marion Brenner
62 (left): You As A Machine, Flickr
62 (right): Jim Choate, Flickr
64: Caitlin Atkinson

65: Félix de Rosen
66: Keeyla Meadows
67 (top): Caitlin Atkinson
67 (bottom): Lexi Van Valkenburgh
68–70: Yann Monel
71: Dan Keck, Flickr
72: Félix de Rosen
73 (top): Félix de Rosen
73 (bottom): Ekaterina Izmestieva
75 (top): Marion Brenner
75 (bottom): Terremoto
76: CEphoto, Uwe Aranas
78 (top): Félix de Rosen
78 (bottom): Caitlin Atkinson
80: Félix de Rosen
81: Nelson Kon
82 (top): Félix de Rosen
82 (bottom)–85: Caitlin Atkinson
86: Rebecca Kmiec
88: F. D. Richards, Flickr
89: Leonora Enking, Flickr
90 (top): Peter Burka, Flickr
90 (bottom): Caitlin Atkinson
92–93: David Fenton
94 (top): brewbrooks, Wikimedia
94 (bottom): Dr. Roman Kuhn
96: Caitlin Atkinson
98: Studio Nomad
99–103: Caitlin Atkinson
104: Keith Michael, Flickr
105: Marie Hervieu
106: Christopher Baker
108–110: Benjamin Vogt
112–13: Terremoto
114: Benjamin Vogt
115: Wagon Landscaping
116: Emanuel Hahn, Wikimedia
118: Clive Nichols
119–20: Félix de Rosen
121 (top): K M, Flickr
121 (bottom): Félix de Rosen
122 (top): Félix de Rosen
122 (bottom): George Stacy
125: Kaldari, Wikimedia
126: Louise Hislop, Flickr
128 (top): MaFe Gonzalez
128 (left and right): Félix de Rosen

130 (left): Félix de Rosen
130 (right): Esther Westerveld, Flickr
130 (bottom): K M, Flickr
132: Félix de Rosen
133: Lutz Heidbrink, Flickr
134: Guilhem Vellut, Flickr
136: Yann Monel
138 (top): Félix de Rosen
138 (bottom) and 140: Clive Nichols
141–42: Félix de Rosen
143: VirtualWolf, Flickr
144: Esther Westerveld, Flickr
147: Benjamin Vogt
148–50: Stephen Powles
151: USDA NRCS Montana, Flickr
152: Felix Niederwange
153: NRCS Oregon, Flickr
154: Teresa Grau Ros, Flickr
155–56 (top): Félix de Rosen
156 (bottom): Susan Gottlieb and Scott Logan
158 (top): Staffan Cederborg, Flickr
158 (bottom): Profaniti, Flickr
160 (left): Michael Panse, Flickr
160 (right): onnola, Flickr
162 (top and left): Charlotte Joubert
162 (right): Félix de Rosen
164: Peter Morgan
165: Félix de Rosen
166–70 (left): Yann Monel
170 (right): Dan Keck
172–73: Félix de Rosen
174: Stacy Levy
176: Elizabeth Frazer
177–78: Center for Neighborhood Technology
179: Félix de Rosen
180 (top): Steve Droter
180 (bottom): NRCS Massachusetts, Flickr
181–83: Curtis Quam
184–85: Félix de Rosen
190: Charlotte Joubert

Published by
Princeton Architectural Press
A division of Chronicle Books LLC
70 West 36th Street
New York, NY 10018
www.papress.com

ISBN 978-1-7972-2244-8

Editor: Jennifer Thompson
Designer: Natalie Snodgrass

Names: de Rosen, Félix, author.
Title: A garden's purpose : cultivating our connection to the natural world
    / Félix de Rosen.
Other titles: Cultivating our connection to the natural world
Description: New York, NY : Princeton Architectural Press, 2023. | Summary:
    "Through stories and essays, A Garden's Purpose invites readers on a
    journey to understand gardens as places where we build mutually beneficial
    relationships with the living world around us" —Provided by publisher.
Identifiers: LCCN 2022028054 | ISBN 9781797222448 (hardcover) |
    ISBN 978-1-7972-2413-8 (ebook)
Subjects: LCSH: Gardening. | Landscape design. | Human ecology.
Classification: LCC SB472.3 .D42 2023 | DDC 635—dc23/eng/20220722
LC record available at https://lccn.loc.gov/2022028054